Crying Loud
and
Sparing Not

EDGAR MEEKS

ISBN 978-1-64114-687-6 (paperback)
ISBN 978-1-64114-688-3 (digital)

Christian Faith Publishing, Inc.
832 Park Avenue
Meadville, PA 16335
www.christianfaithpublishing.com

Printed in the United States of America

John Lawrence
July 14, 1929–September 7, 1985

Foreword

by Bishop George Dallas McKinney
Biography of Evangelist John Lawrence

We initially met each other thirty years ago at a missionary conference sponsored by InterVarsity Christian Fellowship, and Campus Crusade for Christ in Atlanta, Georgia. An insatiable desire to be fully enlightened concerning the legacy of his maternal grandfather, the late Bishop John L. Lewis of the Church of God In Christ in Southern Arkansas, led Elder Edgar Meeks to call me two years ago. I felt there was a sense of urgency as I made several phone calls, and gathered information of people he could speak to once he got to Arkansas. Edgar Meeks followed up by interviewing these individuals, and he paid a visit to one of the churches his grandfather built, spending time with the leadership and various members at Lewis Temple Church Of God In Christ in Texarkana, Arkansas.

The telephone conversation with Edgar Meeks led to a discussion of our spiritual journey. I discovered that Elder Meeks spiritual mentor was National Evangelist John Lawrence. Evangelist Lawrence was an anointed Evangelist who was mightily used in the United States, Africa, and Haiti. His ministry flourished after he completed his Bible training at Zion Bible Institute.

My heart was made glad when Elder Meeks informed me that he had collected many of his messages preached at the great revival of 1984 in New York at Bethel Gospel Tabernacle, pastored by Bishop Roderick Caesar Sr. It was reported that over 500 souls were saved, and 250 filled with the Holy Ghost. Many miracles were reported, whole families were saved, marriages were rescued, and revival fires were started throughout the New York and New England area.

Elder Edgar Meeks has rendered a great service to the body of Christ by preserving and compiling the information so that our generation and generations to come can be informed and inspired by the life and ministry of International Evangelist John Lawrence. From the time of his acceptance of his call to the ministry, to his death in 1985, he did not deviate from his primary purpose, "to know Him and make them know." He was called to be a soul winner. He was not ashamed to engage in sharing his faith with family, friends and strangers. He constantly trained those who he won to Christ to be soul winners also. He was an effective teacher, powerful preacher who always proclaimed Bible truth with practical application. In his preaching and teaching he did not compromise with worldly philosophy and modern theology. He remained faithful to the Bible, the doctrines of sanctification, and holiness. His life was an open book, his relationship with his wife and children was transparent so that his teaching about faithfulness in marriage had a "ring of truth."

It is my prayer that this book will be read by aspiring evangelists, missionaries, pastors, and servant leaders who need encouragement, renewal, and will be refreshed and strengthened to stay in the race. Our congregation was enriched by the ministry of Evangelist John Lawrence. His book will be required reading for all preparing for ministry.

Bishop George D. Mckinney, Ph.D., D.D.

"Come on and stand with me. Lift your hands and say, 'Thank God for Jesus.' Thank you, Jesus. You are the Lord of regeneration; Lord of the resurrection. God, even though we may die, you have made the promise that those who are in the grave will hear your voice and have the hope that Jesus Christ is going to resurrect us from the dead. Father every man, every woman, every boy, and every girl, this day, you've said to them that Jesus Christ is Lord.

"He is the Lord of repentance, and if you will allow Him, today, He'll grant repentance to you. John 6:65 says, "Therefore I have said to you that no one can come to Me unless it has been granted to him by My Father." Jesus Christ has to give you that repentance. If He doesn't give it to you, you'll never repent. And He's offering it to you now. He cannot guarantee you'll have tomorrow. He cannot guarantee you'll have it just before you die. He said, 'Today, if you would hear my voice, harden not your hearts.' (Psalm 95:7, 8) Father, today you are speaking to every sinner, backslider, hypocrite, every man, woman, boy, and girl in this audience. You're saying, 'Jesus Christ, my son, is Lord. And through Him, He offers repentance to you today.' Through Him, you are offering regeneration today. Through Him, you're offering righteousness today. Through Him, you are offering the promise of resurrection. But if you reject Him, you will be damned. You have no hope in this world or the world to come. Lord, have mercy here today. Touch the heart of every man, every woman, every boy, and every girl. Touch the heart of every backslider, every hypocrite, and every person out of fellowship with God today. Convict them of their sins and the works of the power of the enemy. Let them repent right now.

"Every sinner, every person not right with God, every backslider, I want you to lift your hands and say, 'Preacher, pray for me. I'm not right with God. If I die right now, I'll go to hell because I've made no preparation for eternity. Jesus Christ is not my Lord. I haven't repented of my sins. I haven't been made righteous by Him. If I die right now, I have no promise of being in the first resurrection.' You say, 'Brother Lawrence, I've joined the church.' That's not enough. You've got to be born again. You say, 'I'm a pretty decent person.' That's not good enough! You've got to be born again. I'm not asking you to join the church. I'm asking you to let Jesus Christ become your Lord today, to let him rule over your life, and to take control of you! You're here today, and God is stretching out his hands. Tomorrow you may be in judgment. Hell is hot, and eternity is a long time!

"Father, in Jesus's name, every sinner, every backslider, every person that's out of fellowship with you today, Jesus Christ is not their Lord and not their Savior. I pray for them right now. I pray that you'll forgive them of their sins. I pray that you regenerate them. O God, convict them of their sins, their wrongdoings, and change their life. Make them righteous, godly, holy! Bring them to the foot of the cross. Let them accept Jesus Christ as their Savior. Then give them the promise of the resurrection. They will be in that first resurrection where the righteous will get up, children of God get up, and those with hope get up. The last resurrection is for the damned. When they get up, it's too late to do anything but cry! Too late to do anything but scream. For God's mercy will be clean, gone forever. God's grace will be clean and gone forever! There will be nothing or no one you can appeal to! There will be no need to cry for mercy, for mercy will have stepped aside, and justice will be sitting on the throne. No need to be talking about forgiveness because forgiveness will have gone out of business. It will be too late to be forgiven.

"God, have mercy today. Father, in the name of Jesus, I pray for my brother today. O God, have mercy on him today! Forgive him today! Regenerate him today! Make a child of God out of him today. Supernaturally, I pray in Jesus's mighty name. I break the power of sin, the power of Satan, every habit and addiction, and I command a deliverance in Jesus name."

John Lawrence would make a similar appeal at the end of each revival sermon. Bethel Gospel Tabernacle's revival of 1984 began in January and ended in April. It was, as Bishop Caesar Sr. would put it, John Lawrence's "swan song." Night after night, the power of God was immense. John shared his experiences, beliefs, convictions, visions, and the great work God wanted him to do. The thought occurred to me that someone should write a book about this great evangelist. I mentioned this idea to John, and he responded by saying, "Well, maybe you should do it." I smiled and told him I can write music, but I didn't know anything about writing a book. He then suggested, "Pray about it, and see what the Lord says." I took his advice and prayed about it. Three days later, there was a letter in my mailbox inviting me to become a writer through Writer's Digest School. Akin to King Belshazzar observing the fingers of a man writing on the wall of his palace, I considered this a clear directive from the Lord to write this book (Dan. 5:5).

I started the process of writing this book with my first and only interview with John. It was centered around that great four-month revival of 1984. A few months later, I gave him a copy of that interview. He was very pleased. We were supposed to meet again for more interviews, but his health began to deteriorate and we never got together again. The Lord called him home.

The ministry of John Lawrence was anointed, and powerful. Through his ministry God was glorified, the church edified, and thousands of souls were added to the kingdom of God. The Lord led me to incorporate the content and style of John Lawrence's preaching and teaching from that great revival of 1984. In this book, you'll find portions of his opening prayers, sermons, altar calls, and opinions on many topics. I pray that this book will bring pleasure, glory, and honor to God. May it also bless the body of Christ and bring souls into his Kingdom.

The Sound of His Voice

IT WAS DURING A SUNDAY morning service when he made that unexpected visit. As he walked toward the pulpit, a percussive praise of handclaps began to crescendo quickly through the congregation. A conquering hero was marching through the canyons of Bethel Gospel Tabernacle. An overwhelming sense of godly gratitude filled the sanctuary as he sat down with the other ministers. John, who had been very ill, was once again in our midst. I can remember how youthful his appearance was that Sunday morning—much like it was when I first met him forty-seven years ago at Bethel's yearly midsummer revival.

On a warm summer evening, my friend Peter Harris and I were carrying our instruments into St. Albans Plaza. John Lawrence was to deliver the spoken word, and our gospel group was responsible for the ministry of music. I often heard my friends, Peter and his brother David, imitate his rugged, tenacious style of preaching, but this was my first opportunity to hear him in person.

We proceeded to a small room, located on the right side of the stage. Inside, a tall gentleman was putting on his shirt and tie. He greeted us with a warm smile. "Hello, boys. How ya doing?"

Peter responded, "We're doing fine, Elder Lawrence. How are you?"

He said, "Just fine, fine. You boys are playing tonight?"

We both responded, "Yes, sir."

I didn't hear anything unique about his voice during our greeting. It wasn't until he started preaching that I heard that distinctive sound. It was grandiose and forte! My two friends, Caleb Harris and David Anderson, were listening intensely, occasionally smiling and even laughing at the humor in John Lawrence's illustrations and stories. To this day, I can't remember the theme of his message, but I remember the *sound* of his voice.

John and I

J OHN LAWRENCE LOVED HIS WIFE dearly. He made this comment during one of his sermons: "My wife and I have given our whole lives to the Lord's work. We've kept nothing for ourselves. We've never had anything. We've hardly bought anything. I thank God for my wife. No other woman would have lived with me under those conditions."

I will always cherish the time spent with Bernice Lawrence as she shared precious memories of her husband.

"John was born on July 14, 1929, in Greensboro, Georgia, and was the oldest of four children. His parents, Mel and Mary Lawrence, moved their family of four to New Jersey when he was about thirteen years old. I was about eleven years old when I first met John. He was originally invited to our church by the pastor's son, Kelmo Porter Jr. He started attending Sunday school and enjoyed it very much. His fondness for Sunday school was due in large part to the Sunday school teacher, Deacon Patrick. Deacon Patrick took an interest in the well-being of all the boys in class, teaching them about the scriptures, as well as how to dress and behave properly.

"As a young teenager, John was sort of withdrawn. The children his age didn't like him because his complexion was fairer than theirs. He was light-skinned, and the rest of them were dark-skinned. They also felt he was unattractive, just tall and homely looking. Because the rest of the young folks didn't like him, I didn't like him either (laughing), but he enjoyed coming to church because the church leaders and other adults liked him and took much interest in him. As for me, it wasn't until he got saved that my affections for him began to grow.

"John gave his heart to the Lord at the age of fourteen. His best friend, Kelmo Porter Jr., just simply said to him, "Oh come on, John, let's get saved." The two of them gave their hearts to the Lord the same night, but John also received the baptism of the Holy Ghost that very night. John was more serious than Kelmo, so it took his friend a longer period of time to be filled.

"We attended different schools. Therefore, I would basically see him at church functions. He was a fair student who had no interest in sports but loved to read. Graduating from high school was the most gratifying moment in his life. His parents, especially his mother, were very, very pleased.

"After graduation, John continued to be active in Sunday school, Young People Willing Workers, and Tuesday night youth services. His testimonies were short, fiery sermons, and even then, you could see he was powerfully anointed. He began speaking at district and state meetings, and when he spoke, it was *electrifying*. The word got around quickly that there was an anointed young man, full of the Holy Ghost and on fire for God. John would encourage people, pray for people, and the Lord would heal them. Many times, people would come to John with their problems or prayer requests, and God would send answers, healings, and deliverances amid these conversations.

"At the age of seventeen, he accepted the call to the ministry and enrolled at Zion Bible Institute. Zion's policy prohibited students from going off campus during their first two years. When they finally allowed them to go off campus, John would always find a church service to attend. He didn't have a car, so he would walk all over town until he found a church. His testimonies during the devotional services were so explosive that the pastor would have him come back to preach at a future service. Word got around quickly that there was an anointed young man of God at Zion Institute. John's rise as a dynamic preacher was rapid, and he accepted preaching engagements from all over the New England area. During his four years at Zion, he ministered to churches of all denominations and sustained a continuous fellowship with many of these churches throughout his life.

"In 1952, the Lord led him to Atlanta, Georgia. Atlanta was the scene of John's first post-Zion Institute revival. He had just graduated, and while attending a state convocation held by the Churches of God in Christ, Bishop O. M. Kelly spotted him in the congregation. He said to the other preachers, 'Hey, that's John Lawrence. He's a good man. Give him a chance (preach).' One of the elders, George Briley, who happened to be going away on a weekend fishing trip, asked John to preach at his church—Jones Avenue Church of God in Christ. John spoke Friday, Saturday, and Sunday. When the pastor returned, the church was on *fire*. John, under the command of the Holy Ghost, ordered the church to go on a fast, and what began as a weekend appointment turned into a thirty-day revival. The Lord told John to leave after thirty days. Once word got around about the revival, John began receiving many appointments to preach. These revivals, which began as weekend appointments, would often last two or three weeks.

To thank you
for your kind
remembrance.

Rev. & Mrs. John A. Lawrence

"We were married on July 18, 1953, at the Salem Baptist Church in Jersey City, New Jersey. After we were married, John was ready to resume evangelizing. His father, however, thought since I was a registered nurse, I should stay home and make money. But John said, 'No, I want my wife with me.'

"In spite of the fears I had for the South, Jim Crow laws, and lynchings, my first trip with him was to Louisiana. John's first revival lasted for three weeks. It was originally scheduled for one week, but the Lord just kept saving and saving. He had many appointments back then. The revivals would last a week or two and then he would come back home and rest for a week. After a period of rest, he would head out for his next appointment.

"Over the next seven years, the Lord gave John appointments all over the nation. A number of these appointments became established relationships, which lasted his entire life.

"A young teenager named Ernestine Cleveland invited us to California to run a youth revival. John was so effective that her father, Bishop Cleveland, invited him to run yearly revivals at his church. Each year, around the New Year, John ran a revival at Bishop Cleveland's church. He touch many lives during these revivals, and one of the lives he touched was Edwin Hawkins. Before Edwin became a superstar in gospel music, he was a member of Bishop Cleveland's church. John would always give him advice and encouragement and compel him not to sell out to worldly music.

"John developed one of his most important relationships with a church in Chicago at Bishop Goldsberry's church. He was invited by a woman who worked for the Home and Foreign Missions Department. She invited John to speak at a service. The bishop was so impressed that he invited John to speak each year during the month of August. In terms of ministry, this church had the most enthusiastic workers. John had them doing everything: soul winning, jail ministry, street witnessing, door-to-door witnessing, and marriage seminars. In fact, members of this church have continued working as a part of the John Lawrence Evangelistic Team."

Bethel Gospel Tabernacle and John Lawrence

NO OTHER CHURCH, HOWEVER, HAD the kind of history with John Lawrence as Bethel Gospel Tabernacle located in Jamaica, New York. His wife made this comment: "John respected Bishop Caesar Sr. more than any other man of God."

I interviewed John before one of the services during the great revival of 1984. He shared his views on his long relationship with Bethel.

"Twenty-five years ago, I was invited to Bethel Gospel Tabernacle for the first time. An elder's daughter invited me as a speaker for a Youth for Christ service. Pastor Caesar heard me and invited me back for a two-week revival. After a few days of consecration, the revival began. God began to breakthrough and bless so magnificently that the revival continued for about ten weeks. We then left and returned for another two weeks. According to the church's statistics, there were approximately 295 souls saved through that revival. This was a marvelous outpouring of the Holy Spirit. Pastor Caesar and I agreed we've never seen anything like it before. People were praying and getting their families and friends to attend the revival services. God saved entire families. Young men and women were being saved. It was just a supernatural outpouring of the Holy Ghost that started Bethel on the high road to the flourishing and spiritually sound church it is today.

"According to Pastor Caesar, Bethel's membership wasn't very large at that time. However, this revival brought in hundreds of people, especially young people who had new, fresh ideas, which could be put to good use. At this point, Pastor Caesar, being a man of the Spirit, followed the leading of God and wouldn't allow me to leave. I had appointments all over the country and had to cancel every one of them. God did this because He was preparing Bethel and I for a continuing fellowship that would last for the next twenty-five years.

"I thank God for this because Bethel is the kind of place that challenges you to preach your best at all times. You just can't come to Bethel and preach any kind of mediocre sermon. You've got to dig real deep and bring out your very best. They demand and inspire you to give them the best and even above that which you thought was your best. The singing of the choirs, along with Pastor Caesar's great preaching and teaching, creates an atmosphere that rejects any excuse for not giving your best.

"Many ministers such as Moses Taylor, David Smith, and others were products of that first revival. It was a sovereign move of the Holy Spirit that produced such good fruits. I believe God was breaking through in the black church and showing them that if you're willing to pay the price by fasting and praying, you can have a mighty revival. That revival became a standard by which men, women, and evangelists measured revival within the last twenty-five years."

Those Who Knew Him

Bishop Roderick Caesar Sr.

S HORTLY AFTER THE DEATH OF John Lawrence, I interviewed the founder of Bethel Gospel Tabernacle, Bishop Roderick Caesar Sr. at his home in Hollis, New York. I asked him to share his thoughts about John Lawrence, his impact on Bethel Gospel Tabernacle, and the great revival of 1984.

"I discovered that his purpose and objective with the ministry was in harmony with mine. He was a man out for winning souls 100 percent. In that sense, he was a genuine evangelist, and our overall objective in Bethel has always been, and still is, the salvation of souls. So we had a beautiful and harmonious relationship along that line. As you know, he was a man who prayed. He was a man who was very zealous and really 100 percent. He was a man who put everything he had into what he was doing. Not only did he preached; he also gave seminars, tarried with those seeking to be filled with the Holy Spirit, and prayed for the sick—an all-around evangelist. And so we kept having him come year after year. In the sense of soul-winning, he was by far the most outstanding and by far the most profitable evangelist to the church. He had no comparison where that was concerned! He was unique."

I asked Bishop how the revival John held in the 60s compared with his last great revival held during the first four months of 1984.

"It wasn't as large, there weren't as many people, but the spirit was the same. That last one was the climax—his swan song."

I told Bishop I had never experienced anything like the revival of '84. He replied, "I've been pastoring for over fifty years, and my testimony is the same. There never was a second person like John Lawrence. No, he was just unique. A man like that doesn't come along but so often, I'd imagine. No, he was really a man sent from God. I've never experienced any other evangelist like John."

Reverend Joe Little

In October of 1948, John Lawrence along with his good friend Joe Little went to Providence, Rhode Island, and enrolled in Zion Bible Institute. He began witnessing to the lost immediately.

On the first day of their arrival, around five or six o'clock in the evening, John turned to his buddy and said, "Let's go meet the governor."

Joe replied, "The governor?"

"Yes, the governor," said John.

"But you gotta get an appointment to see the governor," Joe answered.

"No, no, let's go," said John.

Joe retorted, "The governor won't even be there." But John wouldn't be deterred, and they proceeded to the governor's office where they were received graciously by Governor John O. Pastori. John presented the governor with a small copy of the New Testament and witnessed to him. Even then, his main and *only* goal was winning souls for Christ.

John was loved by many people, and for the next three years, John and Joe ministered in churches of diverse dominations through-out the New England area. According to Joe Little, it was during these years at Zion that John's vision of starting a world outreach ministry in Atlanta, Georgia, was born. "He was always talking about starting this ministry in Georgia," Joe recalled. It was a vision that was manifested much later in his ministry.

The friendship between John Lawrence and Joe Little would last for years. They were best men in each of their weddings. Joe is godfather to John's oldest son, David, and John was godfather to Joe's oldest daughter. As young preachers, they ministered to neighbor-ing communities around Zion Institute. They ran revivals together and separately for various church dominations: African Methodist, Episcopal, Baptist, Church of God in Christ, and so forth. Some of their professors, those who were also pastors, would invite John and Joe to preach to their congregations. These invitations were oppor-tunities for them to preach to people of different ethnicities. Joe had a smooth, refined style of preaching. John's style, according to Joe's interpretation, was like a *hammer*.

"We had styles that complimented each other, but his preaching was phenomenal. He was very consecrated, always praying. Every morning, he would get up and go to the chapel to pray. His rela-tionship with the people at the school was great. After the years at Zion, we didn't really see each other that much. He began to evan-gelize all over the country. He became popular both nationally and internationally."

Elder James Lindsey

"In 1957, I was a member of Community Mission Church of God in Christ under Pastor James Hallman," said Elder James Lindsey. "I can't remember if I heard John for the first time at Bethel Gospel Tabernacle or Community Mission, but I do remember him so oriented toward the winning of souls. He did not deal with a lot of foolishness—he got right down to business. He would come in and start the revival with three days and three nights of shut-in. If not three days and three nights, then it would be all-night prayer or he'd put the church on a fast.

"He brought a very simple word to the congregation, but his delivery was powerful. He didn't deal with a whole lot of gyrations and other antics. John got right down to business with the preaching of God's Word. He made it clear and so convincing that he'd question your own salvation. John's words would always cause a person to carefully examine their walk and standing with God.

"John was very much like John the Baptist—he was a 'voice crying in the wilderness.' He was led by the spirit of God, not church denominational practices. Now he was a Church of God in Christ preacher and belonged to the organization, but his first priority was spiritual investment.

"I started pastoring in 1959. John would come to my church-run revivals that would run from five to six weeks in length. He was unique in every sense of the word. He was a soul winner. He didn't concern himself with style. He just took care of God's business.

"While I was pastoring, I had a memorable experience with John. He preached a message I knew was divinely directed at me. He used the scripture text, 'O Jerusalem, O Jerusalem, thou that killest the prophets, and stonest them which are sent unto thee, how often would I have gathered thy children together, even as a hen gathereth her chickens under her wings, and ye would not!' (Matt. 23:97). What the Lord was saying to me was clear and simple: 'I wanted to bless you, but you would not obey.' It was disobedience! I admit

Satan was working against me, and my flesh was in an uproar. I went to the holy convocation in Memphis. Sin began to manifest itself in me, and I remembered John's message. One day, as I was coming out of a hotel, heading toward Mason's Temple, I walked right into John Lawrence. He didn't say anything. He just looked at me and knew I had taken a fall. He never spoke to me about the incident, but he did say to me, 'Those who show mercy, should expect to receive mercy.'

"God used John. When he spoke, the Holy Ghost would be on him so—it was as if a gush of wind was coming forth out of his mouth. He was a man of God and an anointed soul winner."

Reverend Herbert Daughtery

"I met him in April of 1953," said Herbert Daughtery. "I was in the Pevonia Avenue Jail, getting ready to go to court. In February, I had been arrested for armed robbery and check forgery—the latter, a federal offense. Since the age of fifteen, I'd been in the fast lane, progressing from marijuana to heroin. I had been addicted to heroin for about eight years and was a part of the early drug scene in my neighborhood. When I first started using heroin, they used to call it 'hoss.' Nobody knew what it was. I can remember turning myself in, and folks didn't know what to do with me. The only treatment center they had at that time was in Lexington, Kentucky. So there I was, strung out on drugs, looking at hard time.

"My mother had asked John to come and see me. She was attending Gospel Tabernacle Church of God in Christ. We also called it Union Street Church of God in Christ. I was very impressed with his focus on his faith in the Bible. He didn't come from a legal perspective, inquiring about lawyers, judges, and so forth. He dealt directly with the saving power of Jesus Christ. I was immediately struck with his sincerity. I had already begun to do some soul searching. My mother and brother had sent me some religious literature, and in fact, I made a commitment to Christ in February. I mean, I had just hit the utter bottom and knew I had all this long jail time to do.

"I can still remember the text for one of John's sermons. He had just returned from one his revivals, and he was commenting on it. 'My heart was hot within me, while I was musing the fire burned: then spake I with my tongue, Lord make me to know mine end, and the measure of my days, what it is; that I may know how frail I am.' Psalms 39:3, 4 KJV. He continued talking, 'How frail we are, how weak we are as human beings, and how we act sometimes, as though we're going to live forever!' Man, I can just see him now so vividly as I talk about it. John was developing at that time this kind of deep voice with a lot of passion and a lot of sincerity. So he would visit back and forth, and that's how we got to know each other.

"I left Pevonia and entered Trenton Penitentiary to serve my sentence of seven to ten years for armed robbery and an additional two years for the federal offense of check forgery. John continued to visit me in jail, and we even ran a revival at the jailhouse. After getting out of jail, in August of 1958, I knew I had to latch on to John. Each morning, I'd get up and head straight to his house. He was always kind and glad to see me, and I would travel with him. In fact, the first all night shut-in service I had ever been in was during one of his meetings at Bishop Caesar's church.

"Despite serving nineteen months for the government, I was still on parole because I owed the state of New Jersey jail time. To leave the state, I needed special permission from my parole officer. When I told him I was a preacher and was traveling with this man named John Lawrence, he looked at me and said, 'C'mon, don't pull my leg. I've been doing this too long, man!' He didn't believe me, so finally he said, 'Well, bring me the guy.' John accompanied me to the meeting with the parole officer. Officer Hone asked, 'I understand that you want Herb to travel with you?'

"John replied, 'Yes, yes.'

"'Well, let me show you something.' The officer went into his drawer, and pulled out my records, which revealed every detail of each crime I had ever committed. When John finished reading, the officer began to stare at John, as if to say, 'You don't know what you've gotten yourself into.' It was a critical moment because in light of these revelations about my past, the parole officer assumed that John would rethink, or even change his mind about having me around him for this crusade or any other revivals or crusades. But Parole Officer Hone wasn't ready for John's reply.

"I can remember the moment, and the words that came out of John's mouth as if it had occurred yesterday.

"'Listen, I'm not concerned with all of that.' John replied sharply.

"'The only thing that I'm concerned about is that this man has an *experience* with God!'

"The officer put the books away and sheepishly answered, 'Okay.'

"Once I began pastoring, even though we didn't spend as much time together, John continued to play a large role in my life. There were some financially lean times during the early part of my ministry. I can remember one night when my wife and I were broke and didn't have enough money to buy food or milk for our baby. I remember searching for pennies along the streets and sidewalks of Brooklyn, hoping to find enough money to buy milk for my baby girl. I eventually found about twenty-four cents and borrowed twenty-five cents from a man I'd met once in my travels around town. I went to the store and purchased a quart of milk and a package of hard doughnuts. I gave the baby the milk, and we ate the doughnuts. The following day, John Lawrence paid us a visit. At that time, he was driving a gray Oldsmobile. He came by, sat for a while, looked around, and finally said, 'Let us pray. Father God, in the name of Jesus, bless this young man.' He left, and came back the next day with his car trunk full of food. We didn't know where he got this food from. We just towed all of it into the house. From that time on, the Lord began to bless us."

Bishop Walter Gibson and Mother Vera Gibson

"We were saved under his ministry in 1957. It was a July revival, which was held at Bethel Gospel Tabernacle. It was near the beginning of John's ministry at Bethel. He was about twenty years old then. My sister invited me. She kept saying, 'Come, there's a young man preaching, and I know you'll enjoy it.'

"I said, 'Well, okay.' So I went and, of course, it was so good that I went every night that week.

"Each night, my sister would say, 'Why wouldn't you get saved? Why didn't you go up and give your life to the Lord?'

"I gave her some reason, but on Friday of that same week, I told her, 'I don't want to get saved and my husband not be saved. That's what you did.'

"She said, 'No, no, no, no. I got saved because my marriage was already bad.'

"I said to her, 'Well mine is good, and I don't want to mess it up.'

"Then she said, 'Well, you better go ahead because you can die and go to hell. He can get married again, get saved, and go to heaven while you'll be lost.' Now that really got to me.

"We lived in the Bronx at that time. My husband was in the Navy, and he was stationed in Little Creek, Virginia, but he came home every Friday. I didn't mention anything to him that Friday, but on Sunday, I asked him if we could go to my sister's church in Queens. He agreed, and we drove out to Jamaica, Queens.

"We sat underneath the balcony. My husband sat in the first seat, and I sat in the second. John preached his sermon and made the altar call. He was making a long appeal for souls to come to the Lord. I sat there with my eyes closed for about fifteen minutes. I was so scared to go up because I didn't know if Walter would accept me getting saved. Would he leave, or maybe I'd never see him again. We had been married for only nine months at that time, so basically, we were still newlyweds. Finally, I said to myself, 'Well, if I lose him, then I'd just lose him, but I gotta go to this altar.' We were sitting right next to the left aisle of the church, so instead of going down that aisle, I joined the group of people who had assembled down the middle aisle. By the time I got to the altar, there was only one person left there. It was Walter. He had left my side and had gone on down that aisle to get saved. Because I was sitting there so afraid, I didn't even notice it. That's how great the power of God was in convincing souls during John's altar calls."

"The one thing I loved about John," said Walter, "was his ability to convince men of their need for Jesus Christ. It was 1958, and I was in the Navy when five of my comrades, who were on their way to New York, had just gotten killed in a car accident. It was amazing the way the Holy Ghost used John Lawrence to express, 'Life is so short, and you can suddenly be gone.' He continued on and said, 'But give Jesus a chance in your life.' It was those very words that convinced me to give my life to Christ. John also said this, 'I'll make you a deal. Just try Jesus, give him a chance, and if you don't like what he's doing, then you can always go back to what you were doing.' I instantly got out of my seat, went down the aisle, committed my life to Jesus, and for the past forty years, I've been walking with the Lord. John made the gospel so plain and simple. He didn't mess around with a whole bunch of words. He was direct and to the point. It was plain and simple to understand."

"The Holy Spirit used him mightily in those days. He was young and dedicated to winning souls for God. The anointing on John Lawrence was so powerful that he would light up like a light bulb. This anointing came as a result of him living a life that was above reproach. John would tell them, 'You need to get saved and get right with God, or else you're going to hell,'" says Mother Gibson. "His words were direct, pointed, and anointed."

"God used John to seal my destiny of being called to the ministry," said Bishop Gibson. "I was fighting with the call to become a preacher for three years, but the fight came to an end during the January revival in 1960. Brother Lawrence had finished his sermon, and he made the altar call and prayed for everybody. He then turned the service over to Bishop Caesar and went into the office to change his clothes. As I was sitting in the pew, I prayed and said, 'Now Jesus, I'm going to settle this once and for all. If you're really calling me to preach, if you want me to do it, you let John Lawrence *come back* out of that office and lay hands on me.' I then went immediately to the altar.

Evangelist John Lawrence

"The moment I got to the altar and closed my eyes, I felt John Lawrence's hand on top of my head and heard the words coming from his mouth, 'Father God, in the name of *J-eee-sus,* bless this man, Lord!' My heart almost jumped out my chest. From that moment on, I accepted the call to preach, and John became a tremendous blessing in my life.

"He didn't preach for profit. It didn't matter where his appointments came from. John preached in storefronts, waterholes, whatever. Wherever there was a need, John would preach. John would not get involved with the raising of money because he had seen so many preachers who started out with an anointing but lost it due to their desire for money. Money was never an issue, especially back in the 50s and 60s. Black people didn't have much money back then, so John would often bring home seventy-five to a hundred dollars a week, and sometimes, not even that much. He would preach a whole week and get three dollars. John, and especially his wife, suffered greatly because of his dedication to the winning of souls. Being a soul winner wasn't lucrative at all, and he spent a great deal of his time away from his children. It wasn't until later in life, when his boys were becoming teenagers, that his wife asked him to come off the field full-time. He became an assistant pastor to his father, and from there, he began planning for the opening of Soul Winner's Institute in Atlanta, Georgia."

John was hurt deeply when he was trying to open Soul Winner's Institute. He had a vision of opening the institute to train men and women as soul winners and eventually send them out as harvesters of souls. Mother Gibson declares, "Entire churches were built as a result of John Lawrence's revivals. When it was time for these churches to support his work in Atlanta, only a few answered the call. He made a nationwide appeal to the throngs of churches he had ministered to, but their response was disturbingly poor. John would say, 'I spent all of these years building your churches, and now, when I need your help, you offer very little of nothing.' Some of these pastors offered these excuses—'Well, things are tight' or 'We can't fit it into our budget.'

"'If it wasn't for the ministry that the God gave me for you, you wouldn't have a budget.' What John wanted to do was come off the field, stay in Atlanta, and build the institute, but he couldn't because he didn't get the support from churches.

"John would have built a tremendous church had people supported his vision. He had helped pastors build their churches across the nation. To John, money was never a problem. He'd go anywhere. Back in those days, black folks didn't have much money. If you came out of a revival with a hundred dollars, you were rich! Most of that money was used on travel expenses. Sometimes John would be on the road for three or four months and then come with only three or four hundred dollars. Thank God Bernice was a nurse. She suffered tremendously for the sake of his ministry and paid some big prices in being submissive to the call on her husband's life.

"Many preachers from his denomination tried to get John to change his style of preaching. They told him, 'You're always beating them down and telling them they're going to hell. You've got to learn to make gravy. You've got to make the people shout. You gotta moan a little bit. Get the folks excited.

"John would reply, 'Listen, that's not me! Man, I'm after getting souls saved.'

"One of the things I loved about John was he wouldn't get involved with their money because he had seen how men started out so anointed but because they got slick and strange about their money, the anointing left. Back in the early days, the pastor would take an offering for the church and then take up the speakers' offering. Well, you know what was left for the speaker—practically nothing! Nobody ever thought, 'Let's take some from what he raised for us and give it to him.' Then other evangelists started changing. They said, 'Let me raise my offering, let me make an appeal, or allow me to pass out special envelopes.'

"John would not go that route. I'd say, 'John you've got to do something. All the rest of your colleagues are.'

"Then he would tell me, 'They gave me fifty dollars.'

"I'd say, 'They gave you what?' This is what they would give him after running a revival for four weeks—fifty dollars! I've seen him cry after ministering in Chicago. They just didn't give him enough money. Sometimes they would just take his money out of the offering he raised. For example, John raised five hundred dollars, and the pastor would only give him two hundred dollars.

"You see, this type of ministry that John had prevented him from being rich. Had he launched into other stuff, he could have raised more money, but he would never do it. All he wanted to do was save souls. People within his own church denomination tried to persuade him to change, but John wouldn't do it. I remember John telling us about a group of women in California whose main goal was to destroy preachers through sex. They've got the money, the clothes, and the appeal to set preachers up and destroy their credibility. John told us of his encounter with one of them. This woman appeared to be very spiritual, and each night of the revival, she would give a hundred dollars in the offering. On the last night of the revival, she made up a story that she needed him to come to her house to elaborate on a theme of a previous sermon. 'Please come by my house to teach me,' she said.

"So John said, 'Well, what time do you want me to come?'"

Mother Gibson states, "He eventually set an appointment to go over there. When he got there, she was dressed in a negligee set, but it was closed up. John went in and sat down on a chair in the living room, and she sat on the couch. As John began to discuss the Word, she asked him to come over to her and show her where it was in the Bible. Well, John was naive to her chicanery, so he went over to her to show her. In an instant, the woman put a bear hug on him so tight that he couldn't get loose. He wrestled and tussled with her, but he couldn't get free. John never met a woman with that kind of strength. He said to her, 'Look, woman, get off of me.'

"She said, 'Look, if you don't give in, I'm going to tell everybody we did have sex. If you give in, I won't tell nobody, and it will be just between me and you.'

"Finally, the Lord spoke to John and told him to pretend he was going to yield to her advances. John said, 'All right, all right, you win, you win, you win! Now listen, if we're going to do this, let's do it right. Let me get these clothes off. I can't do nothing like this.' As soon as she let up just a little, he flew out the door. John would often say, 'When you're out on the field evangelizing, keep your wife with ya because these women out here are crazy!' He'd tell you, 'Be careful when a woman places her offering in your hand instead of placing it in the offering plate. Watch that. They're up to something. She'll tell you the Lord told her to give it to you personally and that you don't have to mention it to the pastor. Watch that. They're not for real. Their lustful spirit will follow their money.'

"We were young in the ministry, but through John's own personal experiences, God was preparing us for the evangelistic ministry. The Lord had told him, ten years prior to the completion of the book, that he would give us a total revelation in the ministry of deliverance, but the churches would not accept it. John knew the ministry of deliverance was right.

"Once the books were in print, John felt led to take copies of the book to his revivals to sell and promote the ministry of deliverance across the country. He'd say, 'Man, this is some good stuff! Everything in here is true. I deal with it every day!'"

The Great 1984 Revival

"While in my travels here in America, Africa, and over other parts of the world, I had become depressed, discouraged, and disappointed. I was feeling this way because I have not seen the kind of revival I saw twenty-five years ago. I thought to myself that perhaps I'd never see that kind of revival again, but several years ago, my wife and I received an invitation to go to Israel. In our first night in Jerusalem, the Holy Spirit began singing out through me: "A mighty revival is coming this way." It's an old song that goes: "A mighty revival is coming this way, coming this way; keep on believing, trust, and obey a mighty revival is coming this way." These words just poured out of me through prophecy, songs, tongues, and interpretation all night long."

Finally, at about five o'clock in the morning, I awoke my wife to pray with me. After we prayed, I looked out over Jerusalem—what a fantastic sight it was. Our hotel was located on a hilltop, and it was just before the break of day. Oh how beautiful it was! As I was beholding the beauty of Jerusalem, the Lord spoke to me and gave me the promise that a mighty revival is coming this way. He also said, "I haven't given you the office of a bishop or any of these kind of positions because I've chosen you for revival. I've chosen you to bring revival to my people."

Later on, during the evening, God said something to me that frightened me. He said, "The church wasn't ready for the rapture." I thought if anybody was ready for the rapture, it would be the church.

It seemed logical to me that since we were saved, we at least would be ready for the rapture, but He continued by saying, "It was not only the laymen. The preachers weren't ready either." Then He went on and said even I wasn't ready for the rapture.

"Well," I thought previously, "if the preachers weren't ready, surely I was." Now don't get me wrong. God didn't say we weren't saved, but as a bride, we weren't complete in our adornment. We were not wearing every part of the bride's outfit. We're not ready to walk down the aisle to meet the groom. This is the state of total readiness that the Lord wants us to be in. Our readiness should be to the extent that we don't have to put on another piece of garment. All we have to do is walk down the aisle and meet the groom.

The church, preachers, and I are not ready to take that walk down the aisle. The Lord said we must first begin our preparation by fasting and praying in a supernatural way. He then told me to come back to America and get four hundred persons to go on a forty-day consecration of fasting, praying, and reading the Word of God. Reading the scriptures, fasting, and praying were the three things that would get the church, preachers, and myself ready for revival. God said the revival would start in Atlanta, Georgia, and spread throughout the South and around the world.

In July of 1983, I was in New York for revival, and Pastor Caesar asked me to come back for Christmas. This revival was originally supposed to last for only one week. I started not to come. I was tired, and I was concerned with getting the revival started in Atlanta so it could be a blessing to the South and to the whole world. But the Lord saw things in a different way, and my wife and I started up to New York.

While we were driving up, the Lord told me to ask one hundred persons to fast and pray with me. They are also to meet at the church at seven o'clock each night of the revival. The people responded wonderfully. Each night, they were at the church, crying out before the Lord for revival. This is the reason why God allowed the revival to break out in the way it did. The people had been praying and fasting for years. They were praying that God would send a mighty revival. The prayer band, led by Sister Williams, had been praying for at least twenty-two years, and this is why the blessings of God is upon Bethel. It's impossible for a church to pray and for God to not answer the prayers.

God broke through! At the end of the first week, there were at least fifty-three souls that were saved and baptized in water. It was during the first baptismal service that the Holy Ghost swept through the service, and revival broke out in a supernatural way. Thus the Lord ordered another week of revival. At the end of the second week, eighty-one souls were saved and baptized. Once again, during the baptismal service, the Holy Ghost moved mightily. The people were just jumping, shouting, and rejoicing. I had never, in my life, seen anything like it. The place was going wild, and for the first time in my life, I saw more men than women being baptized. Never before had I seen such a sight. There were husbands, wives, brothers, and entire families getting baptized at this service. Oh, it was just a fantastic moving of the Holy Spirit. It wasn't John Lawrence who was doing it but the sovereign move of the spirit of God. It was the Lord's doing, and it was marvelous in our eyes. He just took the revival and carried it on, and to Him belongs the glory.

Bishop Caesar had asked the Lord to let him see an outpouring of the Holy Ghost. He wanted to see many people filled with the Holy Ghost in a remarkable way. On a few occasions, there would be one or two who would receive the baptism. However, Pastor Caesar wanted to see a tremendous outpouring of the Holy Spirit. As the revival went on from week to week, there was an incredible outpouring of the Holy Spirit. In one of the choirs, every member was filled with the Holy Spirit. There were some very instrumental altar workers who prayed with these seekers until they received Him. Individuals like Eugene Harrison, the church organist, were very helpful in praying and working at the altar with those who were seeking for the baptism of the Holy Spirit.

God did something very unique during this particular revival. He led me to pray with each individual before they went to the altar. This would often shake or stir them up. The altar workers would have an easier time with them because of this. It was a new kind of approach to my ministry. Many times, an individual wasn't willing to get saved or delivered, so after I took their hand and prayed with them, the spirit of God would break them down, giving them the desire to be saved. As I mentioned earlier, many of those who came to the altar were men. I'd never seen more men than women at the altar during revival. It had always been my desire for God to save the men. If you saved the men, you would often get entire families through the men. It's also my desire to have more men than women in my church in Atlanta. I'm just sick and tired of seeing churches with predominantly women in the congregation. I don't believe it is God's standard. I believe this lack of men problem can be remedied. The blame for this shortage of men should fall on the church and the preachers. For I've seen, in this revival, a complete reversal of this condition.

Another fact I have witnessed in this revival is over one hundred persons had received the baptism of the Holy Ghost. Now this is unheard of. Each week, people were being blessed and healed of tumors and sickness. Families were even brought back together after years of separation. There was a testimony of a boy and girl coming back to their family and back to God. Prior to the revival, they had ran away from home. Now that's a sovereign move of God. There was a case of a husband and wife who had been divorced for nine years. Before the revival, the wife had no desire to go back to her husband, but as a result of this revival, God has saved the husband. He and his wife have decided to remarry and restore their relationship as husband and wife. God challenged all the women to go get their husbands. A great number of them obeyed, and the Lord wonderfully blessed them because of their obedience. Many of them realized they had to first change their ways in order for the husband to get saved. God has specifically dealt with rebellious wives. As the wives showed their obedience, the Lord was able to save their husbands.

Our last service was on Easter Sunday. There were four services on Easter—the last one being a baptismal service. The final count was in: five hundred souls had been saved, and over one hundred persons had received the baptism of the Holy Spirit.

This revival has been the most fantastic revival I've ever witnessed. It lasted throughout the entire winter. That fact alone was incredible. In spite of the cold and adverse weather conditions, the revival was never cancelled on any night. People came to the revival regardless of the weather conditions. I actually believe God didn't allow the weather to get bad enough for cancellations. I believe He kept the winter reasonably tame just for the sake of this revival.

God had let me know we're living in the end times, and time is running out for the church. So with the end time so close, God is pouring out his spirit on many young people and raising them up to minister in a supernatural way. The harvest is so vast that God is calling all of us to use our resources toward God's work. Many ministers and preachers have disregarded the laymen as having actual ministries, but the fact of the matter is, every child of God is in the ministry. We all have a specific duty to accomplish. Whether it's preaching, teaching, or soul winning, we all have a part in the ministry. Therefore, God is equipping his people for the ministry. This is another fruit of the revival. God has captured a great number of young men and women who will never be the same. Many of them are now enrolling in Bible school to prepare for the ministry.

Pre-Sermon Prayers

"**C**ome on. Let's stand and praise God for his goodness. Thank ya Lord. Thank ya, oh God, for your goodness, your mercy, your grace. Thank ya for your salvation, your deliverance. My God, my God, my God, thank ya for the extended time to get right with God. For the extended time to get delivered from sin. For the extended time—God, we thank you! We earnestly and sincerely worship you and adore you 'cause you're wonderful. We thank ya for the harvest. All of these two weeks, we thank ya for the harvest of souls. Men and women, boys and girls, who've knelt at this altar and cried out, 'Jesus, I want you to be my Lord.' We thank you for those who've been baptized with the Holy Ghost. And God you've ordered us to go forward, go on!

"We pray that this week will be greater than any other week—in souls, in baptisms, deliverances, supernaturally—by the power of God. In the name of *Jee-sus*, convict sinners of their sins. Drive the nail of conviction into their hard hearts, and God, let them repent of their sins and come and cry out to Jesus Christ, 'I want to be saved.' Have your way here tonight, anointing the Word by thy divine spirit we pray. And God, you've said it tonight, 'Please don't let this harvest pass!' God, don't let a sinner in this building get out of here until they say yes to you. If they start for the door, knock them down while going toward the door. If they even try to get out of here, slay 'em in the seats, slay 'em in the aisles, slay 'em, my God, going toward the door! 'Cause you're warning every sinner, 'Don't let this harvest pass and your soul be lost at last!' Convict every sinner. Let them repent of their sins and receive Jesus Christ as their Savior so they can rejoice with the saints, in Jesus's name, Amen.

"God is answering prayers. In fact, the only reason this revival is going on is because y'all prayed. How many of y'all prayed? Well, you see, you've got me in trouble because you've been praying. I was suppose to be in Winston-Salem, North Carolina, with Bishop John Hines. We've put it off for one week, and we had to put it off another week. Coming up here, I felt the Lord saying, 'Stop in Winston-Salem, North Carolina.'

"When we got there, Bishop Hines began to pray, and he prophesied and said, 'Brother Lawrence, God is going to anoint you as he anointed you in your youth.'

"I said 'All right, Lord, do the best you can' because I was tired. I was just hoping to get through one week and get out of here and go back to where I came from. But he prophesied and said, 'The Lord is going to anoint you greater than ever before.'"

Prayer from the Fifth Week

"Come on, and let's stand and praise the Lord, for we have been redeemed. Hallelujah, God, we thank ya! Oh, we praise you tonight, for we have been redeemed! Praise God, we've been redeemed by the blood of the Lamb! We've been redeemed by the Savior. We have been redeemed by the Son of God. We have been redeemed! We're grateful Lord. We're thankful. My God, my God, thank yo-o-u that we have been redeemed. Yeah, thank yo-o-u that we have been washed in the blood of the Lamb. Thank yo-o-u that we've been made children of God. My Savior and my God, thank ya Lord! Thank ya for these five weeks of the outpouring of the Holy Ghost. This is the Lord's doing, marvelous in our eyes. To Him alone belongs the honor, the glory, and the credit. For no one but our God could have done this thing these last five weeks.

"Thank you for the souls, Lord. Saved, sanctified, baptized with the Holy Ghost, healed, and delivered. Glory to God. Thank ya, my Savior! Lord, keep on moving, keep on working, and keep on pouring out your spirit in a supernatural manner. We'll never ever forget. I pray in Jesus's name, bind every devil and demon, wicked, contrary and argumentative spirit, and every religious spirit in the name of Jesus! I demand them to be loosed, leave here, and cast out in the name of Jesus. God, we pray for the conviction of the Holy Ghost. Every sin, every habit, every wrong thought, action, or deed that we're guilty of—convict us, convert us, and take control over us.

Lord, we want to be ready when you come back. That sinner, that backslider, that hypocrite, that man, woman, boy, or girl who is not right with God, that person that's about to make a serious mistake—arrest them, Lord, in the name of Jesus Christ, our Savior and Lord!"

Throughout John's ministry, he dealt with many topics in his seminars and sermons. Here's a few topics he addressed.

God Forbids Us to Let
Sin Rule Our Lives

"I heard the spirit say something to me today. I was thinking about a person, and the Lord said this person was married to their sins. If you're married to your sin, get a divorce and get a deliverance."

My brother-in-law Gerald got saved in the 1984 revival at Bethel Gospel Tabernacle. In his own words, he said, "I went to the altar to get prayed for. I wanted God to do something for me. I didn't go up there to get saved, but I didn't want to do any arguing with John Lawrence. So I let him pray for me, and he sent me to the altar. I knelt down at the altar, and I heard the voice of the Lord so clearly. I mean, audibly, the voice of God in my right ear. And He said to me, 'I'm not doing anything for you until you come home.' At that very moment, I raised my hands and asked the Lord to come into my life, make the crooked places straight, fix what is broken in me, and save me. God, just save me! That's all I asked of Him. I know that my hands were up, and I was crying. I don't know what took place for about an hour after that."

Well I do, and what I observed during that hour was incredible. I have never ever seen God deal so thoroughly with a person at the altar. God was literally washing him of every sin he had ever committed and wringing them out of him on the floor of the altar. His countenance and skin color changed while God was dealing with him at the altar. The Lord turned him inside out. When he tried to leave the altar, the power of God would rope him back in. When God finally released him, he was on "cloud 99" for months after.

Marriage

"God knows what to do and whom to give you to. The important thing is waiting until God gives you the right person and until it's God's time. If you wait until God gives you the right person and until God gives you the right time, you won't have to do anymore waiting. If you jump ahead of God and grab something, that's just your grab that you grabbed.

"You may say you're already divorced. Well, God can put it back together again. Where God is blessing, the soul is being refreshed. We are going to be praying for those women who are ready to be married. Now you may be of marriage age and still not ready for marriage. Now I tell any woman, if you can't cook, then you're not ready. You ain't ready for no husband if you can't cook for him. Forget it! Go get you a cookbook, and learn how to cook seven different kinds of meals. Then come back and see me and then I'll pray for you. If you're grown and don't know how to cook, there's something wrong with you and your mama! You're a grown woman and can't cook. There's something wrong with both of y'all!

"I'm going to tell you, very earnestly, if you're not ready for marriage, God is not ready to give you anyone. If you're not ready to love, don't bother. 'Well, I ain't going to love nobody.' Well, don't bother, and don't come up to get prayed for. You need a deliverance! You come at another time! If you're not ready to be led by a man, don't come up. 'Ain't no man goin' to lead me.' Well, don't come up for prayer. Don't bother me because God ain't going to give you nobody. You want to lead him, and that's contrary to God's order. Y'all looking funny already.

"I mean it! If you're not willing to be led by the man God gave you, don't come up. And I'm going to tell some of you, that's the reason God hasn't given you someone yet. You have said to yourself, 'Ain't no man going to tell me nothing. No man is going to lead me! I got more sense than all of them!' Whether you've got more sense or not, when you get married, you come under the leadership of that man. Now if you don't want to do this, then don't ask God to give you a husband! He's not going to do it. If you want to live your life contrary to His Word and His will, don't ask God for a husband. Unless you're willing to be led by that man and come under his leadership, don't ask God for a husband! I'm not saying you can't make suggestions and discuss certain things with him. However, when he makes those final decisions, you must support those decisions.

"All these fellas are thinking about marrying you. Don't marry nobody until you check with the Lord! Don't marry nobody until you check with your mama! Don't marry anybody until you check with their background. A lot of marriages are breaking up because the man has the wrong spirit. Jealously, lust, violence—if you've got these kind of spirits, you'll tear your marriage to pieces. You need to sit down with that fella and find out where he comes from. I wouldn't want to marry anyone without knowing where they come from.

"'Where you come from?'

"'Oh, somewhere in Brooklyn.'

"'No, I want to know where in Brooklyn? Whatcha been doin' all these years?'

"'Well, I've been floating around.'

"Listen, you gettin' ready to tie yourself up with a person for the rest of your life! Your offspring will be born of this man. You don't know what he is, who he is, or what he has done? Some of you better be careful because you may be marrying a criminal. You need to find out and ask him, 'Do you have a record anywhere except in hospital or in the medical center where you were born? I have a right to know.' You better know what you're doing and who you're doing it with. Don't marry anybody until you know everything about them. I tell you something else, don't marry anybody until you go to that background to find out what he or she is, who he or she is, and how he or she is. 'Well, I don't think that's none of my business.' You will think it's your business once you get into that mess, and want to get out of that mess.

"A friend of mine was getting ready to get married to this man. Someone had prophesied to her, telling her it was all right to marry this person, but I take my impressions and leadings from the Lord. This man was from Milwaukee, so I told her I was going to call out there to get more information on this man. I called out there, and nine out of ten people told me to tell her to run for her life. Now the folks out in Milwaukee ain't crazy! If those people who are from the area this man came from told her to run for her life, you'd think she'd listen. She went ahead and married this person anyway! Three years later, the man threatened to kill her. She grabbed her child and ran for her life. She's been running ever since.

"This is one of the questions you young people should ask the Lord before you get married—'Lord, will this person take my life?' Especially these folks who get mad and the first thing that comes out of their mouth is 'I'll kill you! I'll kill you!' If the person you're thinking about marrying says that to you, run for your life! I wouldn't marry anyone who threatens to kill me before I get married to them. Ain't no way you can make me marry that person. The first time he or she says something like 'Listen, don't you play with me 'cause I'll kill you,' consider it as a warning and run for your life.

"The other night, during the service, the Holy Ghost said to a young girl, 'You've got a ring. Now give it back.'

"The girl responded by saying, 'What do you mean give it back? He gave me a diamond ring.'

"'Give it back!' said the Lord.

"Later on, after the service, the girl came to me and said, 'I've got a ring, but the Lord wasn't talking to me.' She hid the ring from her mother and father. Now if you've got to hide the ring, then there's something wrong with whole deal! The ring should be something you're proud of, wanting to show it to everybody, but if you've got to hide it, then there's something wrong with the deal from the beginning. And if there's something wrong with it from the beginning, it's going to be a mess in the end!

"If God tells you 'Don't put your life with that person's life,' listen to God. Listen to God! If you defy God, I prophesy here tonight, you will never be happy. The relationship will never work! There will never be any peace, there will never be any joy, and there will never be any happiness. The devil creates a lust that feels like love. He'll make you believe that it is love. Sometimes it's just the person controlling your life. The devil creates an emotion that feels like love, but it lasts no time at all. Real love comes from God. Real love is peaceable, righteous, and pure.

"The Lord has spoken to our hearts and said that a lot of folks need to be delivered from spirits, attitudes, and habits that are destroying marriages. Some of our emotions are controlled by demonic forces and spirits. The devil won't even let you love or share yourself with your mate. You need a deliverance! To me, it is ridiculous to get a divorce and pay somebody to break up your marriage. It's stupid, as far as I'm concerned, to pay somebody to break up a marriage that you promised God you'd stay in until you die. I think some of y'all were lying anyhow. To tell you the truth, I don't think you ever intended to stay in it until you die, but I believe God can solve your problems."

New Converts

"The greatest miracle God can perform is saving a sinner out of his or her sins. The majority of mankind doesn't know where they came from, who they are, and where they're going. That's why they get drunk. That's why they take drugs. That's why they jump out of windows. They don't know! But when you come to Jesus Christ, he'll tell you where you came from, who you are, and where you're going! He'll put purpose in your *life*! All of you who got saved last week, this week, or recently, please get the baptism of the Holy Ghost right a way. That's the first order of business.

"There's a difference between someone getting the Holy Ghost and someone getting a good blessing. Sometimes people will tarry. They get a blessing, and they feel good and say, 'I got it.' I remember running a revival in Patterson, New Jersey, when a man came off the street and got saved. He immediately jumped up and said, 'Reverend, I got the Holy Ghost.'

"I replied, 'No, you don't have the Holy Ghost. Come on back, and get it tomorrow night.'

"The pastor of the church said, 'Shhhh, that's one of the worse men in all of Patterson, New Jersey. If he said he got the Holy Ghost, let him have it!' No, he don't have it. I ain't gonna tell no lie and tell him he got it. He don't have it. When you get the Holy Ghost, you will speak in tongues or you'll prophecy. There has got to be some supernatural sign aside from you 'feeling good.'

Get the baptism of the Holy Ghost! Don't let any devil, any feeling, or anything stop you. Get the baptism of the Holy Ghost because He'll reveal God's will to you, open the Word of God to you, and give you power to do God's will, and that's important. When the Holy Spirit fills your heart and your mind, Satan is no match for you and God's Holy Spirit. That's why I urge every new convert, don't stop until you're filled with the Holy Spirit. Being saved is all right, but keep on going until you get it all. When you get the Holy Ghost, that puts *power* in your life su-per-na-tur-al-ly! The devil can't do nothing with a Holy Ghost–filled man or woman who's under the control of the Holy Ghost. You're a failure in life without the power of the Holy Ghost. Life will trip you up, knock you down, and run over you like a steamroller, but, brother, when you've got the power of God in your life, you can stand up to life, overcome life, and master *life!*

"All new converts should attend the new convert's class. Get in there, and learn what you should do. All new converts oughta begin going to Bible school. God can't do very much with ignorant folks, but when you know God's Word, God's plan, and how to work with God, he can make you a mighty instrument in his hand.

"When I first got saved, nobody was saved in my family. I went to my mother, father, sister, brother, uncle, aunt, grandpa, grandma, and told them all, 'You better get saved or else you're goin' to hell and burn forever and ever and ever!' I scared the devil out of them, and they got saved. That wasn't the best method, but it was the only method I knew. And it got results! Out of the group came at least five preachers who pastored a half dozen churches. This was all because in my zeal, I shared with others the gospel of Jesus Christ!"

Unbelief Leads to Death

"I heard someone say, 'Well, I just don't believe it.' Your unbelief is what's gonna kill you and send you to hell. You will be bound hand and foot, cast into hell and outer darkness, and throughout all eternity, you're gonna weep, grit your teeth, curse and swear, plead, and pray in vain. It's not because God's wants you to go the hell—he doesn't. God doesn't want a single soul to perish. He doesn't want a single soul to be lost. He doesn't want a single soul to go to hell. The devil and his angels are the only ones God wants to go to hell. You go to hell because you climb over God's mercy. You go to hell because you climb over God's grace. You go to hell because you climb over God's son, the Holy Ghost, his will, and the preaching of the gospel. You get that! You get that!

"'Who does he think he is, standing up in the pulpit and talking to me like that? I don't believe what he says.' That's why you're going to die in your sins. It is not because God hasn't warned you. It is not because God has not spoken to you. It is not because God hasn't dealt with *you!* It is because you say, 'I will not believe it!' Well, this is what God has told me to tell you, 'If you will not believe, then you will die in your sins.' Not because God isn't merciful, not because God will not forgive, but because you will not believe!

"The secret to receiving God's blessing is believing God. You may not feel him, hear him, or understand him, but if you believe him, you can get whatever God has."

Make Sure of Your Calling

"Every child of God has a call. Some people say, 'Oh, Brother Lawrence, I believe in Him, but I'm just not willing to do what He wants me to do. I'm not willing to give up my job.' If God wants you to give up your job, you either give up your job or God can put your whole company out of business. Now I'm not talking to those individuals who say 'Well, I'm going to quit my job 'cause I feel the Lord is calling me to preach.' Do you have a way to make a living, especially if you've got a family to support? 'Well, the Lord is going to make a way.' Listen, you keep on working. If you've got a ministry and folks are calling you to preach and minister, then that's fine 'cause you got a way to support your family, but if no one knows you and no way is made to support your family, you keep on working.

"I'm tired of hearing these lazy folks say, 'The Lord told me to quit my job.' Whatcha goin' to do? 'Well, I'm just going to stay home and meditate.' No, you just goin' to stay home and *sleep*. God ain't in that. If God called ya to the ministry, you ought to be in school or ya oughta be working with somebody who's in the ministry and witnessing every day.

"If God asks you to give up your job, he will always send a witness. If God speaks to you, check it out with another child of God. If God has told you to do it, he will give you a witness. Someone will confirm it. If you have no witness and no confirmation, don't make a

51

move. The devil will ruin your life, tear up your home, break up your marriage, and mess up your future!

"'Well, I know the Lord.' No, you don't know the Lord. You know that something, some voice, some spirit spoke to you, but what voice and whose spirit? Stay on the altar until God sends a witness! You've got to be sure it's God! He'll give you confirmation out of his Word, through a witness, and sometimes through a small miracle or wonder. If you want to find direction for your life, you must fast and pray. Then God will give you direction for your life. God never fails to answer the prayers of those who will fast and pray."

Preaching According to God's Command

"Some people say, 'I don't like the way John Lawrence preaches because he's always preaching doom and judgment.'

"I preach doom and judgment because that's what the Holy Ghost has preached to me. I preach doom and judgment because on my knees, I say to God, 'Give me a word!'

"He'll say, 'This is the word.'

"Sometimes I'll tell him, 'Lord, I don't want to preach that. I don't want preach doom. I don't want to preach judgment. I don't want to preach death.'

"He'll say, 'You don't have no choice about what you preach.'

"The preacher don't have no choice about what he preaches. Not if he's God's preacher. The preacher must preach what the Holy Ghost gives him to preach. Many times, I'll say to God, 'Lord, I don't want to preach it.'

"Then He'll say, 'Preach it anyhow.'

"I don't like it!

"'Preach it anyhow.'

"The folks may not want it.

"He'll say, 'Who cares what they want. Give them what they need!'"

Seeking God

"If you're going to seek God, you must first give up your sins. God and sin doesn't mix together. If you're seeking God, you've got to turn all the rest of that stuff loose and seek him with all your heart. A lot of people don't get an answer from God because they are not ready to give up their sins. There's no need to be seeking God when you're not ready to give up your sins. God will not answer you. The only answer you'll get will be from one of His thunderers who'll say to you, 'Give up your sins!' Then you'll get mad at him, saying, 'Who does he think he is, telling me to give up my sins?' Well, it's God telling you what you've got to do if you want his answer. If you want His will revealed in your life, you've got to quit doing wrong. Wicked habits, wrong habits—you've got to give them up.

"I remember the story of a man seeking the baptism of the Holy Ghost. I was in a forty-day revival. It was hot down in Fort Myers, Florida. I was tarrying every night with this man, and I got tired of him and everything else. I said to the Lord, 'I'm tired of tarrying with this man. Why don't you give him the Holy Ghost? We've been tarrying for forty days.'

"The Lord told me to go to his house. So I went to his house, and the Lord said, 'Look between the kitchen and the dining room.' So I looked between the two rooms, and the Lord said, 'Now look up.' I looked up and saw old gold Chesterfields. All of those cigarettes were sitting there on the shelf. The Lord said, 'That's what's wrong with him. He won't give up his cigarettes!' So I said, 'Come here, brother. What's this?'

"He said, 'Oh, that's nothing.'

"I said, 'Don't tell me that's nothing. Throw them things in the fire!' He threw them in the fire, and that very night, he got baptized in the Holy Ghost. If you want the Holy Ghost, you've gotta give up everything. God is not going to baptize you with his precious spirit when you haven't given up all of these habits, sanctified yourself, or at least be willing to give up all for him. God will wait until you come to a place where you are willing to do anything, and then God will give you the Holy Ghost.

"If you want God's direction for your life, you must seek him with all your heart. I've watched some of you come up to the altar and seek God for three minutes, then get up and run. Sometimes your prayers are still hanging in the air, and you've gone back to your seat. You ain't gettin' nothin' honey! If you want an answer from God, you need to stay before God, cry out to God, seek God, and wait for an answer. If you want what God has, you have to seek God. You've got to give God time! I fear very much for this generation. They don't want to take time for nothing. Instant love, instant abortion, instant salvation—I hope y'all make it in. When I was coming up—brother—it wasn't just kneeling two seconds down here and then gettin' up. Those old folks put you down there, and they tarried with you, spit at you, hit you. They made gettin' saved such an ordeal that once you got it, you didn't ever wanna lose it again! Now we've got this instant stuff. *Thirty seconds, and you've got it. Thirty seconds later, you've lost it too.* There ought to be a sincerity about seeking God, staying there until you get something from God because it's going take something to stand for God."

Soul Winning

"I believe with all my heart that the greatest work in the world is leading a soul to Christ. That's what Jesus did, that's what the apostles did, and that's what we ought to do. If you have never led a soul to Christ, I feel sorry for you. You have missed one of the greatest joys in the Christian life. When you lead a soul to Christ, heaven shouts and rejoices with you. You should win at least one soul to Christ before the year is out. I challenge you, in the name of the Lord, to win at least one soul to the Lord this year. Really, you ought to lead at least twelve people to Christ—one for each month. I believe it gladdens the heart of God when he sees someone being led to Christ. Men, women, and children can be led to Christ.

"My next stop is Atlanta. God has given me the green light to go ahead and begin training thousands of young men and women for this great revival. I have my sons who are also in the ministry right by my side. They will be assisting me in this great revival. This is a fulfilled promise to me. God said to me, 'I will put my words in your mouth, and in your seed's mouth, and in your seed's, seed's mouth.' God has kept his promise by giving me sons who are in the ministry. My job is to cry loud and spare not. Now is the time to cry loud and spare not in Atlanta, Georgia. I'm not a young man anymore. I have, at the most, fifteen active years left in the ministry. I plan on giving all these remaining years to the work of the Lord in Atlanta. Some of us must realize that this may be the last year for us or some member of our family. I want you to pray and ask God, 'Is there a member of my family who is just one step from death? And if there is, show me that person so I may go to that person and start dealing with them about their soul.'

"We were ministering in Chicago, where we saw God do some great and mighty things, and God spoke to my heart and gave us a new method in dealing with souls. The new method is simple. You go up to a person and ask him or her for directions to a location in town. It could be the police station, the library, or anyplace. Once they give you directions, you say, 'Thank you very much. Now will you please tell me, how do you get to heaven from here?'

"The thing that thrills me is that people start smiling because they realize they don't know how to get to heaven. They'll say, 'Well, uh, I go to church.'

"'I didn't ask you which way to the church. I asked you how to get to heaven from here.'

"Now, the person is caught and condemned by their own conscience. They'll eventually say, 'To tell you the truth, I don't know how to get heaven from here.'

"At this point. you can simply explain to them that it is easy as 1, 2, 3. Acknowledge God as your creator, believe on the Lord Jesus Christ, confess your sins and confess Christ as your Savior, and Jesus Christ will show you the way from here to heaven. God wants us to share what we have with those who have nothing. Any sinner, any backslider, any hypocrite, any person without God have absolutely nothing they can hang on to five minutes after their death."

Parenting

"We ought to teach our children, from the day they first begin to cry, about the God who created them. I believe we ought to let our children know there is a Creator. I don't care what they tell them in school about evolution. Evolution is the biggest lie ever told. Man did not evolve! God created man in his own image, after his own *likeness*. We have to teach our kids, early in life, that they've got a Creator. We got to teach even more than that because people will come up to them and say the creator is Allah. His name is not Allah. I don't know who Allah is, but he is not my Creator. Jehovah is my creator. Somebody said, 'Well, Brother Lawrence, are you sure they're not the same?'

"I know that they're not the same because Jehovah spoke out of heaven and said, 'This is my beloved Son, in whom I am well pleased, and hear ye him.' Allah doesn't have any sons, so they can't be the same! We ought to read the Bible with our children. By the time our children are grown, we should have read the entire Bible to them.

"Children don't understand the price you have to pay to bring them into this world. The thing that breaks your heart is when they get to be about ten or twelve years old, you'll hear them say, 'I'm not goin' to clean no room. I'm not goin' to wash no dishes. I'm not goin' to come in at no eleven o'clock. I'm goin' to come in when I feel like it.' My God! Then they got the nerve to say, 'I'm a man.'

"You don't even know what a man is. You can't take no responsibility, can't even do a job around the house. You won't take the garbage out, you won't scrub the floors, and yet you go around saying you're a man. A man is someone who stands up and fulfills his responsibility. You don't want to wash dishes or scrub the floors? That's all right, just don't eat tonight. We'll exempt everybody from eating if they don't want to work. I'm not going to feed some big fat lazy bum who don't want to do anything. No, sir! Cut off the food and say, 'You don't work, you don't eat!' It won't be long before he or she falls in line.

"Some men don't make any decisions. They'll say, 'Go ask your mama!' No, that ain't the way it ought to be. Mama and I will meet together and then decide what it ought to be. When the kids come to daddy, you, as the father and head of the house, should tell him or her what the answer is. 'Well, my child may not like me.' Like me or not, I'm the head of this house, and you got go by my rule. This ain't no popularity contest to see who can give the child the most and which parent he or she is going to like the most. I'm here to raise you, and I'm going to raise you right—like it or not.

"Some fathers don't want to chastise their children, and they tell their wives to do it. The chastisement of the children should primarily come from the father. Many men don't want the responsibility of making the decisions in their marriage. Marriage is a heavy responsibility, and God is telling the men, 'Carry your part of the load.'

"If any of you young people haven't been pulling your load at home, don't go home and start testifying to your parents about getting saved. Instead, go home, and change your attitude. Go home, and start doing things you have never done before, sharing your responsibilities and helping your mother and father. It won't be long before they start noticing and asking, 'What happened to you? If you can make a change like this, well then, maybe I ought to check out this God you serve.'

"Don't let anyone get between you and your parents. I will let no one make me an enemy of my parents. The mother who brought me into this world, I will never make her my enemy. The man who worked for twenty-one years to help me get by, I'll never make him my enemy. I may get angry at him, but I'll never say a word to him.

I'll walk outside and holler at the wind. I'll never lift my hand against him. Never! I'll never fight him because that's my dad. The Bible says, 'Honor your father and mother.' And God said, 'I'll lengthen your days on this earth.'

"God said this to me, 'John, parents ought to love their children.' A lot of us would have to confess that we really don't know how to love our children. Some of us are selfish and mean, and some of us just don't care. Once you bring children into this world, you now must love them, feed them, cloth them, and teach them.

"A lot of young people are having children and saying, 'Here, Mom!' I believe before almighty God that if you have them, God expects you to mother and father your children. I don't care what you think you're going to tell God during the judgment! You owe those children love, time, and companionship. On Judgement Day we will have to answer to God concerning the raising of our children. Some of our children are going to condemn us. They're going to say to God, 'My mother never had any time for us. My father never had any time for us. We were lonely and heartbroken, and they gave us no time.' Share yourselves with your children. When you share yourself with your children, you'll never lose your children.

"I remember getting off the plane the other day. My son and my wife had driven two separate cars to the airport to meet me. He was standing outside his car while I was getting into the car with my wife. Once I got into the car, I hesitated for a moment and noticed he was still standing outside of his, just looking at me. I began to wonder, 'Why is he just standing there looking?'

"Finally, he yelled out, 'Hey, Dad, you don't kiss your wife anymore when you come home?'

"I said, 'Just gimme time, boy, I gotta get myself together here!' Children expect you to be loving. When you're loving, they become loving."

Father's Day Message—6/84

"A father is one who is concerned for his children. If you're not concerned for your children, then you're not a father. You may have planted the seed, but you're not a father, just a seed planter. A father doesn't just plant the seed and walks away. A father plants the seed and helps the seed to grow.

"I don't know what gives a man the idea that he can go around and have sex with any woman he sees. Then once the woman gets pregnant, they just go on about their business and have no responsibility. That's not true. That's not God's divine will, and it's not right in the sight of God. Some of you girls don't realize the seriousness of the situation. Every man who grins at you doesn't love you. They don't even think much about you and don't want you. They just want to use you.

"Some of you don't realize you're playing with fire. Don't even listen to a man unless he's talking about putting a ring on your finger, a marriage certificate in your hand, and making you his wife for the rest of your life. Some of you say, 'Well, I can handle him.' You're a fool! You can't handle nobody. You may meet a couple of dumb men or dumb boys who don't know anything, but you're going to meet some of them who knows something. When you meet the right one, he's going to turn your head all the way around, sideways, backward, and before you know anything, you will have done something that will mess your life up forever.

"Some of you think your Momma doesn't have good sense. 'My Momma is an old foogy. She don't know what's happenin'.' Your Momma knows what's happening, honey, and she knows what's going to happen if you continue to act like a fool. You'll come home and say, 'Momma, I'm pregnant.' What do you want Momma to do? Some of you want to have a baby and then bring it home to Momma and say, 'Momma, raise my child.' No way! You got him, you raise him. You wouldn't listen, you wouldn't care, you wouldn't take counsel or advice. Now you've got a problem, and it's your problem. You wouldn't go to school before. Now you've got a child, you want to go to school and leave the baby home with Momma. No, no, you've got a baby to raise.

"God told me last night to warn the young women and the young girls that a man is not something to play with. He's not something to play with. He's not a toy. You think it's fun and games, but it ain't no fun and it ain't no game. He is deadly serious! And he'll mess your life up and laugh at you. While you cry your eyes out, while you suffer, and while you go down to the doors of hell, he'll laugh at you and tell you, 'I don't care!' Then you'll have to bear the pain, you'll have to bear the responsibility, and you'll have to carry the load for someone who didn't care nothing about you. God told me to warn you that he has given man an ability to persuade your mind, but this ability was given to him to use on the woman he is supposed to marry, not any just anyone he finds. Only the one he's supposed to marry.

"Now let me say something to you fellas, God is going to make you pay, sooner or later! If you're old enough to be a man, then get you a wife and have a family. Don't slip and slide, mess around here, then plant a seed over there, and once that girl gets pregnant, you'll run over here, and start seeing another girl, get her pregnant, and then you'll say, 'I don't know which one I'm going to marry.' They oughta put some of these boys out of the church. Just put them out of the church until they marry one of them. There oughta be some kind of law, some kind of order, or some kind of standard set somewhere!

"You girls better have sense enough to know that if a boy has messed up a couple of girls, there's no way you should marry him.

God is sick of men who are absentee fathers, plant the seed, walk off, and leave while the child asks the question, 'Where is my father?' The mother answers, 'I don't know where your father is.'

"A real father is someone who is concerned about his children. My wife has every child and every seed I've planted in life. I don't have to say, 'Well, I don't know how many children I have.' I know how many I've got, and the number is seven. I've planted all of my seed in one place. That's what a man will do. That's what a father will do. If there are any here who have made a mistake, and you've got a child, don't tell me about the welfare taking care of your child. You take care of your child! Send that woman money every week to take care of your child because God is going meet you during the judgment. God is going condemn you! You have no excuse for not being concerned about your child. A father thinks about his children. He plans for his children. Sometimes when he can't do very much for himself, he'll do for his children. Tragically, some of the mothers don't even know who is the father of their children. Listen, don't let the devil wreck and ruin your life! Stand up! Learn how to say no!"

Taking Responsibility

"Some of us want to be kids forever. We just don't want to grow up. It's sad that many parents don't force their kids to grow up. They'll say, 'I want them to enjoy themselves.' Listen, there's a time and a place for the good times and enjoyment, but there's a time and place for responsibility and maturity.

"People in the church just want to jump, holler, and run up and down the aisles. That's part of it, but that's not all of it. Praying is part of it. Fasting is part of it. Finding His will is part of it. Seeking the Lord is part of it. Going to Bible school is part it. There comes a time when you must grow up. In the church, grow up and shoulder your responsibility. If you do nothing, when you meet God, you'll receive nothing.

"You ought to grow up in your marriage. It is sad, but some of us men put all of the responsibility on the woman. Some of us marry you good women because you are strong and you look dumb enough to carry the whole load. So we say, 'Here, carry it.'

"There was a time when men would carry the groceries for the women. I see some of these women carrying these huge bags, and the man is carrying some little bag of something. If I was you, women, I'd sit the bag down on the sidewalk and say, 'You either carry it, or you don't eat!'"

Lust

"One of the most important things to remember about lustful desires is the enemy brings them to you, but you only become guilty once you agree with those desires. The enemy will make people believe they are guilty because these desires come in their minds. Lustful desires come to all men and women. You are only guilty when you agree to follow through with that thought or the intent to commit that sin. Don't agree with that thought. Don't accept or allow yourself to become a slave to that thought. As long as you fight against that thought through prayer, fasting, and the reading of God's Word, you will not be guilty of that sin."

Give God the Right Away

"Let Jesus Christ determine your profession. Only Jesus Christ knows fully what he has put in you and which area you're going to be a success in. He knows the gift, the talent, the ability. He knows what you've got! God made you to do one thing, and meanwhile, you're over here trying to do something else. God is saying, 'Fool, you ain't got no sense. That ain't what I made you for.'

"And then you'll say, 'Well, I want to do this.'

"And God says, 'You ain't gonna do nothing but make a fool out of yourself. Instead, do this!'

"And you'll say, 'I don't like that!'

"God says, 'But I gave you the talent for this!' Now I know y'all ain't going to agree with me, but give God the right to choose your partner for you. 'Brother Lawrence, I see this pretty little girl. She is the prettiest thing I've ever laid mine eyes on. Now Brother Lawrence, the Lord said that he will give you the desires of your heart, and Brother Lawrence, that pretty little thing is what my heart desires! What shall I do?' I suggest that you come down to the altar and say, 'Lord, I see a pretty little thing, but is that pretty little thing the one you want me to have?' Don't you go by what you see, because sometimes what you see ain't what you get! These girls have mastered the art of creating an illusion. They say, 'I'm tender, I'm sweet, and just delicious!'

"If you want to know what they're *really* like, go talk to their mamas. Get real close to their mama and say to her, 'Ma'am, I want you to tell me the truth, the whole truth, and nothing but the truth. Is your daughter as sweet as she looks and acts?' Now Mama is caught between a rock and a hard place. If she pleads the fifth, the answer is no! She oughta be able to say, 'Yes, I've got to tell you the truth, my daughter is as sweet as she looks.' That's what she should be able to say because she birthed her and raised her. She should be able to testify for her daughter. If Mama doesn't testify for her daughter, brother, grab your hat, and run for your life!

"It goes the same with the fellas. These fellas are cool, put on these airs, and make you think you're getting a prince when, actually, his horns and hooves are stickin' out. And if you look close enough, you can almost see a tail. Get with their daddy and their family and say, 'Listen, I want to know the truth. Is he really what he says he is?' If anybody asks me, I'm going to tell them the truth. I'm not going to lie for any of my children. Unless I tell the truth, I will become a party to the lie being told. And years later, I don't want anybody to look me in the face and say, 'If you had told me the truth, I never would have married your son. I would have never married your daughter. My whole life has been messed up because you didn't tell me the truth.' Some of these old folks would have to say, 'Amen.' If they had known the truth, they would have never married the person they married.

"Now God knows the truth! If you get on your knees and say, 'Lord show me the partner, the person, I ought to marry!' God will show you that person. Some of us will try to make God give us a particular person. Don't try to make God give you that particular person. Don't ask God for something you know isn't his will—you are asking for trouble. Once God reveals a certain thing is not his will, then leave it alone. 'Well, Brother Lawrence, it will break my heart.' It's better to have a broken heart that God will eventually heal, than get into a situation out of God's will, that he'll do nothing for. If you go against God's will, you will suffer for the rest of your life. So, please, discern if it's in the will of God.

"You ask the question, 'How will I know?' If it is spoken against in God's Word, then you'll know it's not God's will. Don't ask God for an unsaved husband. That's against God's will. 'Well, he's almost saved!' That doesn't count. 'Well, he acts like he's saved.' That doesn't count either. A lot of these fellas are putting on a good front. After they get you, they're goin' to whip your head. Get on your knees!

"One woman said to me, 'Brother Lawrence, I got on my knees, and I asked God. I said, 'Lord, I don't want no divorce. I don't want my home messed up. I want a husband I could live with until I die.' She said, 'I didn't know anything about God, but I got on my knees and asked God for a husband, and we've been married for over twenty-five years. Later, we did get saved, and everything has been so wonderful. I believe if you ask God, he will give you the partner you're supposed to have and live with for the rest of your life.'"

God's Pattern

"Let God give you the pattern for your life. God knows the pattern that will fit your life, so let God select the pattern for your life. God gave me a scripture over forty years ago: 'The just shall live by faith.' That's the pattern for my life—a life of faith. There comes a time when God will prosper you after you've proven to him that you're willing to accept his pattern for your life. It may be the pattern for a missionary life. Some people may say you're crazy and stupid for choosing that pattern. If that's the pattern God has chosen for you, then go to the mission field. If God chooses for you to open up a new work or enter into a new ministry no one else has even thought of, then follow that pattern, and don't let anyone move you from it."

Preparing Your Body, and
Mind for Marriage

"God will say one thing that will change your life. Therefore, it is important to press your way and come out to the special men sessions devoted to preparing oneself for marriage. Every young man thinking about getting married must prepare himself for leadership. A leader is somebody who has a plan that tells them where they're going and how to get there. A fool has no plan, doesn't know where he's going, and doesn't know how he's going to get there. We don't want any fools getting married.

"Last night, God talked about having the right spirit and preparing your spirit for marriage. A lot of marriages are breaking up because the man has the wrong spirit. Jealousy, lust, and violence—if you've got these kind of spirits, you need a deliverance because you'll tear your marriage into pieces.

"Tonight, we talked about preparing your body for marriage. A man needs a strong healthy body. Therefore, the body must be taken care of. If you're sick in your body, go see a doctor. Come up here for prayer, and we'll pray and anoint you. But if nothing happens, make an appointment with your doctor. If you're mentally sick, and some of y'all better watch these folks. There's some crazy folks trying to fool you, and you won't realize it until after you marry them. But if mentally you know there's something wrong, go see a mental health specialist, find out what's wrong and why, and what medication you can take to function right for the rest of your life. I've got several friends who must take medication every day. They're married, but they must take medication because if they don't, they'll go off. Some of them I have to almost beat up verbally to make them take it. I'd rather bully them and make them take it so they can function, than have them go off and be no good to anybody. If you need a certain medication for the well-being of your mental health, you take that medication! Don't let anyone tell you anything differently. They're not sick, and they're not mentally off. You are, and you're the one who needs it.

"Sometimes we ask God for things we're not prepared to handle. Some of y'all are praying, 'Lord, give me a husband.' And once you get one, you don't know how to handle him. You'll say, 'I don't feel like being bothered. I don't feel like cooking. I don't want to clean the house.' Well what do you want to do? If you don't feel like cooking, cleaning house, or making love to your husband, you stay single 'til you die. Go buy yourself a dog, cat, or a parakeet. If you're not preparing to deal with it, handle it, and make the necessary adjustments, don't ask God for it!

"Let me tell you something, if you ask God for it, he gives it to you, and you don't deal with it properly and right, he's going to judge you. And when you stand at the judgment seat of Christ, he's going to condemn you, and you'll be sorry you've ever asked God for it."

Listening to the Voice of a Lying Spirit

"There's a message in 1 Kings 22:18–23: '"Did I not tell you that he would prophesy no good concerning me, but evil." And he said, "Hear thou therefore the word of the Lord: I saw the Lord sitting on his throne, and all the host of heaven standing by him on his right hand and on his left." And the Lord said, "Who shall persuade Ahab, that he may go up and fall at Ramoth-gilead?" And one said on this manner, and another said on that manner. And there came forth a spirit, and stood before the Lord, and said, "I will persuade him." And the Lord said unto him, "Wherewith?" And he said, "I will go forth, and I will be a lying spirit in the mouth of all his prophets." And he said, "Thou shalt persuade him, and prevail also: go forth, and do so." Now therefore, behold, the Lord hath put a lying spirit in the mouth of all these thy prophets, and the Lord hath spoken evil concerning thee.'

"My wife and I were praying for your requests today, and I saw a gambler. And I believe you're here tonight. And the Lord said to me, 'That man, woman, or young person is listening to a lying spirit. Now you're here tonight. You don't know why you're here. You don't know how you got here. You didn't intend to be here. Maybe you were kidnapped, fooled, or tricked into coming here. I've told the saints to get the people in here so you might hear the Word of God for the last time. Now I saw this gambler, and the devil is telling you, 'You're going to win. Play one more time. You're going to win this one. Put up your house. This is a hot one.' Now you hear a voice talking to you. You feel a spirit dealing with you. You're so sure this has got to be real! If you've got the guts to come up here, I will pray for you, but God told me to tell you, you are listening to the voice of a lying evil spirit that will ultimately destroy you. Listen to the voice of God tonight, breakaway, get a deliverance, and save your soul. Lift your hands and say, 'Lord, help that man.'

"Listen to what God told me to tell you. You have rejected the voice of human reason. God gave you parents to tell you what is right and what is wrong. And normally, parents will tell you what is right. Nobody wins at gambling except for the people who owns the business. Don't you know they wouldn't be in the business if they didn't know they were going to win! These business owners are not in business for you to win, and you've got to be a fool if you think they are. They are in business because they know they can't lose! Gambling is a losing business for everyone except the owners. God said to me that you have rejected all human reasoning. Your parents, husband, wife saying, 'Don't gamble all your money up.' You work forty to fifty hours a week to make your little money. The casino owners and workers are home during the day eating and sleeping and get up just by the time you get off work. They get to the casinos and start shuffling the cards, preparing the tables, ready to roll the dice. Within one hour, you have spent your entire weeks' pay, and you go home broke, mad, and full of the devil. You beat your wife and whip your children, acting like you're the baddest dude around. They oughta throw you out the house.

"'Well, I'm the man.' If you're the man, bring the money home. Don't come home with your excuses, saying somebody robbed you, attacked you, and took your money. You're a liar! You put the money on the table! Now if you just got to gamble or you're going to gamble, why don't you have sense enough to just go home and say, 'Honey, here's the money for the rent. Here's the money for the food and so forth.' Then take a little money that's left, go out there, gamble that all up, then come home and go to bed. At least you have paid your bills, bought the food, and put a little bit in the bank. So if you lose a little bit that's left, you don't hurt everybody.

"But a lying spirit is telling you, 'No, no, take all the money. Be a big shot. Show them what kind of man you are. Go up there, and throw it all down. Shoot the roll!' What God showed me, and what's so pitiful about you is this lying spirit is telling you, you're going to win! That spirit knows there is no way you are going to win. A lying spirit doesn't care about you! A lying spirit doesn't have your best interest at heart! A lying spirit doesn't care about your family! A lying spirit doesn't care about your kids! That spirit gets a kick out making you look like a fool! The spirit says, 'Look at you listening to me, blowing your whole roll on one toss of the dice, one spin of wheel, and one pick of a card. God wants to help you tonight. If you don't get help tonight, you may never get help for the rest of your life.'

"I've never preached a sermon like this before, and God has never led me to specifically deal with a gambler. The brother who got up and testified tonight confirmed that this was the move of God. You have rejected human reasoning from your parents, your husband, your wife, your whole family, and even your friends. They say, 'Man, you're a fool! I wouldn't blow my whole paycheck.'

"Then you reply, 'Well, one of these days, I'm going to hit it big. One of these days, I'm going to hit that number, and I'm going to break the bank.' You should live so long. The bank is not built for you to break. The bank is built to break *you*! Then they will loan you money at about 100 percent interest, and tie you up for the rest of your life. You'll never pay off the debt. You'll just keep paying on the interest.

"God said you have rebelled against his voice. You've been taught gambling is wrong. This is even taught in Sunday school. Folks who have children ought to see to it that your children come to Sunday school. There are a lot of parents who don't want to get up early enough to get their children ready for Sunday school, but your children should go to Sunday school. You ought to see to it that they go to Sunday school because there are things they're going to learn in Sunday school that they're not going to learn anywhere else. If you can get them up to go school, you can get them up to go to Sunday school.

"You have rebelled against the preacher. You'll say, 'I don't see anything wrong with it. It doesn't feel wrong. These preachers don't know what they're talking about. There ain't nothing wrong with gambling.' It is wrong to take another man's money and give him nothing in return. It's wrong! It's wrong to take another woman's money, wrong to take food out her children's mouth, and give the person far from an even chance to get her money back.

I think that it's a shame and a disgrace for the state to be in the gambling business. We're producing a nation of gamblers. No good can come out of that. They play up the one person who won five million dollars and say nothing of the five million folks who lost everything. Nothing is said about it, but they'll play up the one man who won five million dollars, saying, 'That could be you!' That's a lie. That couldn't be you. You had about one chance in five million. Anyone with good sense knows that's no chance at all.

"You have rejected the voice of God through your spiritual advisor. God has put a spiritual person in your life. This person will take an interest in you and give you advice, guidance, and counsel. You'll say, 'You know, I gamble a little bit,' and that person will say, 'You shouldn't do that.'

"Ninety-nine percent of the time, you lose! Some of you former gamblers should tell the truth. Ninety-nine percent of the time, you lose! Most of us have gambled at some time, in some form. Only a very few of us has won. Most people lose, but the advertisements make you believe most people win. That's a lie! You are listening to the voice of a lying spirit! 'Well, Brother Lawrence, I hope I'm going to win. If I win, I'm going to pay my tithes.' That's a lie! If you win, you ain't going to pay no tithes! You don't pay no tithes now! If you win a million dollars, you're not going to pay no tithes. That's the truth. If you don't pay tithes out of a couple of hundred, you ain't going to pay no tithes out of a million! The greedy spirit in you is going to say, 'That's too much money to give the church!' Come on, Holy Ghost, help me here tonight. I'm going to make the altar call in a few minutes.

"You've rebelled against the voice of God through the preacher, the prophet, the teacher, and through the spiritual advisor. Let me warn you. God has sent me here tonight to tell you you're listening to the voice of a lying evil spirit, and you're going to lose! Somebody said, 'Brother Lawrence, you know the Lord gave me a number last night.' That's a lie. God does not give numbers, and playing numbers is wrong. Come on, and lift your hands and say, 'Help me, Lord.'

"You've rejected the Word of the Lord that was sent to you. You've rejected the way of God. God's way of holiness does not permit gambling. No gambler is a Christian, and no Christian is a gambler. I know there are churches that finance themselves through gambling, but that's not God's way! God does not approve of churches gambling. 'Well, Brother Lawrence, what about a little bingo?' God does not approve of bingo or any other kind of 'go.' God's spirit does not approve of bingo in the church. These churches are wrong in the sight of God for trying to finance the church through bingo. God said tithes and offerings. If the people of God give their tithes and offerings, then you don't need bingo to finance the church. The Bible says, 'Everyone who is willing, let him bring an offering.' This is what God approves of, and you've rejected that.

"You have accepted the voice of a lying spirit that tells you you're going to win, you can't lose, this is a sure thing—it comes from the horse's mouth. Any fool knows the only thing that comes from a horse's mouth is his saliva. The tip you're getting comes from a lying evil spirit's mouth."

In our text, the king of Judah, Jehosophat, and the king of Israel, Ahab, met. King Ahab gathered four hundred prophets to ask them if they should go up against the Syrians. Ahab's prophets told him to go up against them for the Lord will deliver the Syrians into his hands. King Jehoshaphat knew Ahab's prophets were lying. Jehoshaphat loved God but loved wicked people also.

I want to warn you young folks. If you try to love God and wicked folks also, you're going to lose out. If you love the Lord, stop loving wicked folks. Stop listening to wicked folks. Stop following wicked folks. Stop being partakers with wicked folks because sooner or later, they are going to make you backslide. He asked Ahab was there a prophet of the Lord to inquire of. Ahab said there is one man named Micah who never gives good prophecies concerning him but only evil ones. It's amazing that some will ask for counsel from the Lord, yet they really don't want to hear what the Lord has to say. So King Ahab reluctantly called for Micah. When he gave him the same word as his own prophets gave, Ahab knew he wasn't being honest with him, so he asked Micah to tell him the truth according to the name of the Lord. Micah replied, "I saw all Israel scattered upon the hills, as sheep that have not a shepherd: and the Lord said, 'These have no master: let them return every man to his house in peace.'"

Then King Ahab got mad because Micah was prophesying King Ahab's death. Let me warn you. When God's servant speaks to you and tell you what God said, you better listen! God was giving this man a chance. God didn't tell him to go up there in the first place. That was King Ahab's desire. God didn't send him up there. God didn't command him to go up there and mess with the Assyrian king. That was his desire. God placed the truth into the mouth of Micah. "No, don't go up there, and if you do, you're going to die if you go up there!"

Ahab said to Jehoshaphat, "Did I not tell thee that he would not prophesy good unto me, but evil." This is the point when Micah told him the vision he had of God standing in heaven with rest of the heavenly host. They were discussing that his time had run out and how they would get him to make a foolish move to get himself killed. Many spirits came before the Lord, explaining how they could get to Ahab.

Finally, one spirit stood before the Lord and said, "I will go out and be a lying spirit in the mouth of all his prophets."

And the Lord said, "Thou shalt entice him, and thou shalt also prevail: go out, and do even so."

Now this king could have believed the man of God (Micah). He could have called off the expedition. He could have told Jehoshaphat to go home! He could have lived the rest of his life without dying before his time, but instead of believing the man of God, instead of listening to the Holy Ghost after the man of God told him there's a lying spirit in the mouth of all of your prophets, Ahab told them to lock him up. To feed him with the bread and water of affliction until he returned in peace. He believed the lying spirit from the mouth of his prophets. He went up to this battle.

Now the strange thing about it was he told Jehoshaphat, "I will disguise myself, and go to battle." But Jehoshaphat was foolish enough to go riding into battle with his royal apparel on.

The king of Syria said, "Listen, we don't want to bother any of these little guys. Kill the king of Israel." When the Syrians saw Jehoshaphat, the king of Judah, they converged on him. But Jehoshaphat cried out to the Lord, and the Lord made them depart from him after finding out he wasn't the king of Israel.

The king of Israel was disguised, and no one could recognize him. However, one of the Syrians put his arrow in the bow and, by chance, just shot the arrow. He didn't know, but that arrow had King Ahab's name written on it. That arrow caught him in a vital spot between the joints of his harness. He told his chariot man, "Turn thine hand, that thou mayest carry me out of the host: for I am wounded." He died that day according to the Word of the Lord!

This message was for someone in attendance that night.

John said, "You listen to me tonight! You are listening to the voice of a lying evil spirit. Now I saw this gambler. There's no hope for you in your own will power. There's no hope for you in gamblers' anonymous, by itself. God is saying tonight that your only hope is to come here, kneel at this altar, let me pray for you, and anoint you. God told me how to break that power of gambling addiction over you tonight. You can be delivered! If you do not, that same lying spirit is going to make you commit suicide after you've lost your wife, home, family, children, and everything you got. He's going make you take your own life. And while you're dying and passing from one side to the other, you're going to get a glimpse of that evil spirit laughing at you saying, 'Man, wasn't you a fool! The preacher told you what my job was. The preacher warned you about what I was going to do and about what I was trying to do. He described my method, my procedure—everything! You didn't have sense enough to let God deliver you. Welcome home in hell forever because you listened to the voice of a lying spirit.'"

Many young born-again Christians are negatively influenced by the shaky lives exhibited by older Christians. Young people have a hard time digesting the hypocrisy found in the lives of these Christians. Some of them are their own parents or relatives. They continue to minister in their churches without remorse and are never held accountable for their actions. The young Christian feels if the older Christians can get away with it, then it must be okay for them to get involved with these sinful practices.

John Lawrence said, "I saw some of you young folks listening to the voice of a lying spirit. The spirit that tells you, you can sin and be right is a lying spirit." John continues, "If you sin, you are not right. If you're right, you don't fool with sin! The lying spirit that tells you, you can play with sex and not get caught is a lying spirit. That spirit says, 'Oh, you ain't goin' to get caught. You're too smart.' Well, talk to some of those who are bouncing these babies around here now. They'll tell you that is a lie! They got caught, and will be caught for the rest of their lives.

"The spirit that tells you, you can date an unsaved boy and be saved and stay spiritual is a lying spirit. If you are saved and he's not saved, it won't be long before neither one of you will be saved. This is not only for the young people, but also for some of you older ones too! Some of y'all are playing around, some of y'all are slipping around, and some of y'all think ya slick. Honey, there ain't nobody slick but the devil! Lying spirits that tells you God doesn't mind, or doesn't care, and we can get away with anything. Nobody gets away with sin! The Bible declares, 'The wages of sin is death, but the gift of God is eternal life through Jesus Christ our Lord.'

"Some of you have heard a spirit say to you, 'Go ahead and marry that boy. It's going to work out all right.' You'll say to me, 'Brother Lawrence, the spirit said to marry him.' A spirit did tell you that, but what kind of spirit? I've had young folks all across America tell me, 'Brother Lawrence, something told me to marry that fella, something told me to marry that girl, and it didn't even last six months. Why did God tell me that?'

"Don't put God's name in this. God didn't mess you up. If God tells you it's going to work, then it's going to work! But there are lying spirits that tells you it's going to work even when God's counsel from the pulpit was no! The counsel from your parents is no. The counsel from your spiritual advisors is no. God is not going against all that counsel and say yes. Never! A lying spirit is telling you, 'You go on and marry him anyhow, and you show them that they are wrong.' You're a fool! You ain't going to show us nothing! When the spirit of God says it won't last three months or six months, write it down. It won't last. If the spirit of God tells you, you will not celebrate your first year anniversary, write it down. You won't celebrate one year of marriage. Don't you let the devil tell you that He doesn't know what He's talking about. That's calling God a liar! Then you'll still say, 'Well, I'm going to try it and see.' I wouldn't put my life on the line for nobody! God told you before you got started that it will not work!

"A few years ago, I went to a church to visit a friend. When I got up to say a few words, the Holy Ghost said this to a young girl. 'You're planning your wedding. You've got your bridesmaid and everything together, but the man you're marrying is not saved. He'll never be faithful or true. When you're pregnant with your first baby, he will be going out with someone else.' I didn't know the young girl, and I had no idea who the Lord was talking about. I just spoke the words as the Holy Ghost gave them to me.

"When I went back to the church again, they said to me, 'Brother Lawrence, do you remember the last time you were here, and you spoke that word?'

"I said, 'Yes, I remember.'

"They said, 'One of our girls was getting married, and she got so mad. She didn't know what to do. She got mad at you. She went on and got married anyway, pregnant with her first child, and her husband is running around with other women. Isn't it a shame?'

"I don't have any pity for her. When God tells you a man will not be faithful, you better believe what God said. When God describes in details what's going to happen, you better believe what God is saying. But you'll say, 'Brother Lawrence, the spirit told me I can make it work. I'm woman enough, and I can handle the situation.'

"I agree that a spirit told you that, but it was a lying spirit! You don't know what you're woman enough to do until you get into this marriage deal. Then you'll find out it takes more than a woman. It takes God in a woman, helping a woman, and sometimes they both can't do nothing with that crook. The crook has to be willing to live right and do right in the sight of God, and far too often, he is unwilling to do that.

"Some of you women are listening to the voice of a lying spirit. That man is sweet talking you and telling you how fine and beautiful you are. Believe it if you want to, but God is saying if you're not careful, you'll be listening to the voice of a lying spirit. You'll be risking your life by saying, 'Well, Brother Lawrence, I just want to get married.' No, you don't want to just get married. You want to stay married! You want to be happy while you're married and glad that you married the person you married.

"A lying spirit will make you get married, and then you'll get mad with God. 'Oh God, why did you let me marry this person.'

"God will say, 'You didn't ask me anything.'

"Some of you will bring the man to the preacher and say, 'This is the man I'm going to marry.' You don't ask, 'Pray for us to see if we are supposed to marry each other.' You don't ask, 'Will you counsel us to help us discern if this is God's will.' You say, 'This is the person I'm going to marry.' You set the date and time of your marriage ceremony, and never ask for any counsel. Then, when it doesn't work, you get mad at the preacher and at God. It's not God's fault. It's your fault! Lift your hands and say, 'Lord, don't let me make a mistake.'

"For some of you, it's too late. Just say, 'Lord help me in the mistake I've made. Help me in the mistake I've made because I made it. I rejected your counsel, your Word, and your advice. Now I've got to just suffer through it until Christ sets me free.'

"What are the results of listening to the voice of a lying spirit? You die before your time, you die out of fellowship with God, and you die and go to hell because you wouldn't listen to the warnings of God."

Mother's Day Message: God's Ideal Mother, Sharing Yourself with God and Another

"Father, we want to thank you for we do not believe you have brought us this far to leave us. Hallelujah! We believe, Lord, that you are going to bless us in an unusual and supernatural way. We pray, in the name of Jesus Christ, that this day will be a day we will never forget. As we gather here today, we pray for every mother, Lord, that's in this building and every mother-to-be in the name of Jesus. We thank you for these mothers, Lord, who have carried such a burden and responsibility. We ask the blessings of God upon them and the strength of God.

"Lord, may they continue to obey you and fulfill their responsibilities in the name of the Son of God. Now we pray Lord for those who are sick today. Reach out your hand right now Lord. Touch every sick one in the name of Jesus. Let the healing virtue of the Son of God flow into their bodies right now. In the name of Jesus, let there be a supernatural deliverance, a miracle of our God that's so wonderful and marvelous that we will never forget it as long as we live. Send your Word today. God, grant a conviction of the heart of every man, every woman, and every boy and girl. Every person that has any sin in their life and not right with their God, grant repentance and bring them into the Kingdom of God. For we ask it in Jesus's name, Amen!"

"We thank God for this Mother's Day, and I certainly thank God for my mother. For how she raised me and brought me up in the fear of the Lord. I thank God for my wife, the mother of the seven children the Lord gave me. I only wanted four, but the Lord wanted seven. So we compromised and had His seven. Sometimes God doesn't always give you what you want. He sometimes gives you more than you want. If the Lord giveth, then you better just say, 'Thank the Lord.'

"The Word of the Lord in the Book of Luke 1:26–38 says, 'And in the sixth month the angel Gabriel was sent from God unto the city of Galilee, named Nazareth to a virgin espoused to a man whose name was Joseph, of the house of David; and the virgin's name was Mary. And the angel came in unto her, and said, "Hail, thou that art highly favoured, the Lord is with thee: blessed art thou among women." And when she saw him, she was troubled at his saying, and cast in her mind what manner of salutation this should be. And the angel said unto her, "Fear not Mary: for thou hast found favour with God. And, behold, thou shalt conceive in thy womb, and bring forth a son, and shalt call his name Jesus. He shall be great, and shall be called the Son of the Highest: and the Lord God shall give unto him the throne of his father David. And he shall reign over the house of Jacob for ever; and of his kingdom there shall be no end." Then said Mary unto the angel, "How shall this be, seeing I know not a man?" And the angel answered and said unto her, "The Holy Ghost shall come upon thee, and the power of the Highest shall overshadow thee: therefore also that holy thing which shall be born of thee shall be called the Son of God. And, behold, thy cousin Elizabeth, she hath also conceived a son in her old age: and this is the sixth month with her, who was called barren. For with God nothing shall be impossible." And Mary said, "Behold the handmaid of the Lord; be it unto me according to thy word." And the angel departed from her.' In verses 46–47: 'And Mary said, "My soul doth magnify the Lord, and my spirit hath rejoiced in God my saviour."'

"God's ideal mother is a woman who, first and foremost, shares herself with God. She, unreservedly, makes that commitment early in life. God's ideal woman gives herself to God first. So many women say, 'Brother Lawrence, I don't want to get saved. I want to first get me a husband. After I get me a husband, then I'll get saved.' Let me tell you something. If you don't have God to help you pick out a husband, you will, no doubt, end up with nothing! If you haven't made that commitment to God, don't go any further. Don't do nothing else. Hold everything and do, first things first, share yourself with God before you share yourself with anybody else!

"God's ideal woman will ask the Lord and say, 'Lord, where, and who is the man I'm supposed to share my life with?' This 'eenie, meenie, minie, mo' way of choosing a husband ends up in a mess every time. You'll marry 'Meenie' when you oughta' marry 'Mo.'

"I had a woman who wasn't saved and said, 'Brother Lawrence, when I was a young woman, I was so afraid that I was going to make a mistake and pick the wrong man to marry. So I got down on my knees, and I said to God, 'God, I don't know the right man to pick, but I'm going to ask you to help me pick the right man that I won't have any problems with for the rest of my life.' Brother Lawrence, I wasn't saved then, but God heard my prayer, and sent me the right man. I've been married many years, and since then, I've gotten saved. I have a happy home, and I know that God did!'

"So many young women let their momma push them into marriage. Momma will say, 'Child, you better get you somebody, get somebody, anybody, just get somebody, and get out of here!' Don't you let nobody rush you and make a fool out yourself. When you are picking a husband—next to you getting saved—you are making the greatest decision in your life! You don't get but one chance, usually, to make that decision, so it got to be right. It has got to be right because if it's wrong, you're in hell for the rest of your life.

"God created woman to share herself with man. That was her highest calling. Her body, mind, gifts, talents, all of it is to be shared with her own husband. Sometimes her mind is a little sharper than his. Y'all might as well be honest. I married my wife because I knew she was smarter than I was. I wasn't marrying me no fool! In one sense, I was smarter than she was because I picked her out, and she didn't have enough sense to respond. Running and fussin' and acting a fool. It was only after I got saved that God said, 'Listen, woman, that one is for you.'

"She said, 'Yes, Lord.' For twenty-seven years, we've walked together, loving each other with all our hearts. The Lord said to share your mind with your husband. We men need all the help we can get. Any man who thinks he doesn't need no help is out of his mind. If you've got a good and strong mind, don't try to overwhelm him. Don't try to make no fool out of him! Some of you women say things like, 'That old dummie I've got. Old stupid idiot …' That's why God gave you to him. He needed help! You are the help! So get in there and help! I know I won't have many friends when this sermon is over.

"God made woman to share her body with her own husband. Titus 2:4 says, 'That they may teach the women to be sober, to love their husbands, to love their children, to be discreet, chaste, keepers at home, good, obedient to their own husbands.' Everywhere I go, men come up to me and say, 'Brother Lawrence, pray for my wife.'

"And I'd say, 'What's wrong with her?'

"'She doesn't want to be bothered with me.'

"I looked at him and said, 'I'm going to pray for both of y'all.'

"I heard a story that really broke my heart. A man's wife was so caught up into the church. Every night, every service, she was there all the time. He was sharing this with another man, and he said, 'You know, I've got a good wife, but she's not meeting my needs. She's in the church so much until I think I'm going to have go in the street and get me a woman. I don't want to go out in the street, but I've got to do something.'

"Any woman who refuses her husband is not God's ideal kind of woman. 'Oh, Brother Lawrence, I'm just so spiritual. Oh, my mind is just not on that anymore. Whew! I'm just so heavenly minded.' Listen, I'm goin' to tell you the truth. If you don't come back down to earth, you're goin' to lose your husband, break up your home, and end up a fool at the end. You can speak in tongues, prophesy, but you're just wasting your breath. That ain't God's spirit making you all that spiritual. We use it as an escape and an excuse not to do our duty. You need to be spiritual at the proper time to be spiritual and to be honest at the proper time to be honest.

"If you have a husband, God expects you to share yourself with your husband. 'Well, Brother Lawrence, I don't feel like it.' Feelings ain't got nothin' to do with it. God told me many women don't respond to their husband because they haven't willed themselves to respond. They've never made up their minds and say, 'This is my duty. This is what God created me for, and I'm going to do it to the best of my ability.'

"God said, 'Listen. The secret of happiness is not always having everything the way you want it. The secret of happiness is to accept whatever comes and *will* to be happy in spite of it.' Paul said, 'I have learned, that whatever state I'm in, there with to be content.' Now there's a man who have been beaten, whipped, thrown in jail, and treated worse than a dog. He said, 'I've learned to rejoice.' What he's saying is he willed himself to be happy! We complain about why we're not doing our duties. We'll blame it on him and say, 'Well, the reason why I'm not doing this is because he did this or that, and so forth.' God said, 'The reason why you're not doing anything is because you don't want to!' He told me every woman here should make up her mind and say 'This is why God created me. This is my job. To share myself with my husband.'

"'Well, Brother Lawrence, he ain't saved.' The Bible teaches us that if a woman's husband is not saved, she has to have a meek and quiet humble spirit, be submissive, and obey God's Word and His spirit. That man can be won to Christ without her saying a word! I didn't say it. God's Word said it. Many times the man is not a Christian and doesn't know the deep things of God. Your spirit has found them, and if you share everything, you will share those also. One of the reasons why a lot of our testimonies are no good is we don't share nothing but our testimonies. When you refuse to share anything else, nobody wants to hear your testimony.

"There was a young man who was so disillusioned with America that he was willing to permanently leave this country and move to Canada or some other part of the world. However, he decided to give this country one more chance by walking across the country. He met people in the back woods, across the countryside—black, white, Asian, and so forth. He said the sharing of food, clothing, and every-day necessities from Christians was the single reason that drove him into becoming a Christian. During his cross-country walk, he would often get hungry, tired, and wouldn't have any money.

"It was during these times when a Christian family would see him walking the streets and offer him a ride to his destination. During the ride, they would ask him if he wanted something to eat, and he'd gladly accepted the food after not eating for an entire day. He said, 'When each Christian family, time and time again, shared everything they had with me, it convinced me to accept Jesus into my life.' Some of you have friends, family members, and neighbors you're witnessing to. You're giving your testimony, and they continue to reject your invitation to Christ. Stop giving your testimony, and invite them over for dinner. When they are in trouble, share what you have. It won't be long before they'll ask you why you've been so kind to them, and that will be your opportunity to share Christ with them.

"God's ideal kind of woman never shares herself with her children before she shares with husband first. They couldn't get around having children without a man, so they got married. Once they get the children, the husband is ignored. Now anytime he says to her, 'Honey, can we …'

"You cut him off and say 'I've got the baby' or 'What about the children?' Don't put the children first. Put them in their place. The place of children is after your husband. Many homes break up because the husband sees the wife placing the children before him.

"After a while, the husband will say, 'Listen, I was here before the children. I picked you for my wife, and the children just came on, whether we asked them to or not. They just wandered on in here.' I've seen some mothers come to the table, put the child's plate down, and feed the child before they put their husband's plate on the table. The husband is looking at her saying, 'Where's my plate?'

"She'll respond, 'Well, I want to feed Johnny first.'

"He'll say, 'How come? Did Johnny work today, went hunting, or something?' He gets mad, cuss, and fight, and that does no good. He'll go to the bar and get drunk, and that does no good.

"Then somewhere along the way, he meets a woman who'll say, 'Mr. Jones, you look very lonely. You look like you ain't got a friend in the world.'

"He'll reply, 'I haven't.'

"She'll reply, 'Well, what about your wife Mr. Jones?'

"'Well, my wife is so caught up with the children. I just feel like an outsider.'

"She says, 'Well, Mr. Jones, I know how you feel.'

"'What do you mean?'

"'Mr. Jones, I don't have anyone either. And, Mr. Jones, if you need someone's shoulder to cry on, you can cry on my shoulder.' While he's crying on her shoulder, he's going to grab her, and business is going to pick up! And when you eventually wake up, you are going to be home alone with your children, and your husband is going to be somewhere else. After the children are gone, you and your husband are going to be alone. If you have forgotten how to be a husband and wife to each other, how to be loving, and how to be close, when the children leave, both of you are going to want to leave.

"You didn't make a commitment to your children for life. You have not said 'unto death do us part'! But you've made that commitment to your husband, and you've made that commitment to your wife. So you must remember, twenty or twenty-one years of raising children, and then they're gone to start their families. Normally, there are many years after the children are gone when you and your husband have to live in the same house. Woman, you may not want to hear God, but God is talking to someone! If you've built the right kind of relationship, if you have been loving, if you've been kind, and you have shared yourself, then it gets sweeter and sweeter.

"I read a story, which, in a way, sort of broke my heart, of a husband and wife who had committed themselves to each other. She was loving, kind, and the ideal wife. She caught a disease, and the husband took her to the doctor. The doctor told him there was no hope. He took her to fifty different doctors, and they all said there was no hope. He finally said, 'I'll take care of her myself.' He fed her, washed her, and clothed her. It practically broke his strength and mind. The husband was forced to put her in an institution where she just simply lay, curled up in a fetal position. She couldn't talk and respond to anything, yet the husband went there every day to see her and tell her he loved her. He'd visit her each day, lay his hands on her, and tell her how much he loved her. That's God's ideal kind of husband. She wasn't any good to him at this point. She couldn't serve him any longer, but she had served him in the past. She had shared herself when she was able, and the only thing that he could do now was tell her he loves her over and over and over again. He said, 'I love you for what you have been, I love you for what you have done, and I'm going to be here until you die because that's the promise I made to you.' God commands husbands to love their wives. If they're not loving their wives, they are disobeying God.

"A lot of wives want to stay young and pretty. They don't want to have kids at all. They say, 'I don't wanna lose my figure.' Well, your figure was given to you so you could have children. That's what God gave you your figure for! 'I don't want any children. I just want my husband to adore me, I want to be pretty, I want other men to admire me, and I want to be set on a pedestal.' God didn't make you to be set on a pedestal. God created you to be a help mate and a sharer. I was reading last night about one woman who had twenty-six children. Now I don't mean you should go out and have that many children! This woman had twenty-six children. After the twenty-sixth child, the doctor said she could have some more. So I don't know about her husband, but I know if it was me, I would say 'never.' Never! God knows twenty-six is enough and too much. I'm not saying you have twenty-six, but you oughta multiply a little bit. Once you multiply, you take care of them. You brought them here. You take care of them, you feed them, you teach them, and you love them.

"A lot of our women are having children and say, 'Here, Mom.'

"And Mom says, 'Thank you, honey!' But I believe, before almighty God, that if you had them, God expects you to mother them. I don't care what you think you're going to tell God during the judgment. You had the child, and you owe that child some love, time, and companionship. You are going to need to have an answer for God in eternity! Some of our children are going to condemn us. 'My mother never had any time for me. My daddy never had any time. I was lonely and heartbroken, and they gave me no time!' Share with your children! 'Brother Lawrence, these children get on my nerves.' They always have, and they always will. Handle your nerves the best you can, and get on with it!

"I remember when God spoke to me about taking my family across America. I said, 'Lord, I'm tired all the time, praying for folks and preaching. You can't be serious!'

"He said, 'Yes, I am.'

"I said, 'Seven children in a station wagon. My wife and I are out of our minds already, and you want us to pack them in our station wagon and take them across America in forty days! You've got to be kidding me!'

"He said, 'No, I'm not kidding.'

"I said, 'Okay. Help!' I told my wife. I don't remember what she said, but she has always agreed with what the Lord tells me to do. She works, and she shares with her husband. We got them together, got them into the station wagon, and took them across America for forty days. Now I didn't understand what God was doing, but out of that experience, a ministry with our children developed. They began to minister, and they began to share themselves. Today, four of my children has claimed that God has called them to the ministry. I didn't call anybody, I'm not going to save anyone, and whatever happens, I'm not responsible. I'll help them to do whatever God tells them to do, but they will never say 'My father called me to preach.'

"I pray with them, ask God to make it plain, speak loud and clear, but this is between them. God let me know recently that if I hadn't obeyed him by spending time with my children, they would be out in the world. But because my wife and I shared ourselves with them, they are here. When you share yourself with your children,

CRYING LOUD AND SPARING NOT

you'll never lose your children. When you share yourselves with each other, they learn to share themselves with their wives and husbands.

"God's ideal wife not only shares herself with her husband and children. She shares herself with neighbors and friends who don't have and come to her with nothing. She shares a cup of sugar, flour, loaf of bread, or a piece of meat. She shares whatever she has. When we share, we show the love of Christ.

"There was a man who was in a concentration camp. This man never spoke to anyone. None of the others in the camp ever heard him speak. Most believed he couldn't talk, but there was a Christian who believed he could make him talk. Each day, when prisoners were receiving rations, the Christian would take his portions and give them to the man. This took place every day. He still wouldn't say anything. Eventually, the Christian took sick and died. At his funeral, there were remarks given by different individuals. Finally, after everyone had finished giving remarks, this man who had never spoken before stood up and said, 'This man was more like Jesus Christ than any man I have ever known in my entire life.' We ought to lift our hands to God and ask Him to help us share with anyone we meet.

"As I went over this message at the chapel in prayer, the Lord spoke to me and said, 'Not only mothers, but you and others should share yourselves.' Christians have become selfish. Very selfish. The Word of the Lord spoke to me out of the Book of Luke 9:23–25: 'If any man will come after me, let him deny himself, and take up his cross daily, and follow me. For whosoever will save his life shall lose it: but whosoever will lose his life for my sake, the same shall save it. For what is a man's advantage, if he gains the whole world and lose himself, or be a castaway?'

"I heard the spirit of God saying, 'I want you to share yourself with Christ through the Holy Spirit.' I heard God speaking to my inner man, saying, 'You must share yourself with your wife, your husband, and your children.'

"You may say to the Lord, 'I don't feel like doing it.'

"I hear the Lord saying, 'Will yourself to do it. Will it, will it! Force yourself, if need be, but you must do it!' Share yourself with the unsaved and ungodly. Show them God's love and help them know God! God will show you how, when, and where! The Bible says if your enemy is hungry, you feed him. If they're naked, clothe them. When you do this, you prick their conscience and stir up their memory. They know you're doing this because you are a Christian and you know the Lord! You convict them, and eventually, that conviction will lead them to repentance and God will reward you in the years to come."

Closing Prayer

"Holy Spirit, I thank you for your Word. You did not come to make us happy, please us, make us rejoice, or make us proud of ourselves. You've come to bring us the truth and tell us the truth about ourselves. Lord, we need help today. I pray for every mother. I pray for every Christian. I pray for every sinner and every person who doesn't know God in Christ. You said you created us to share ourselves with you, God, and with each other. Anyone who's not doing this can never please God. You said, 'I've created you to share yourself and not to be selfish.' One of the greatest scriptures states, 'Thou shalt love the Lord thy God with all thy heart, and with all thy soul, and with all thy strength, and with all thy mind; and thy neighbor as thyself.' God, you're gonna have to help us. We need all the help you got to help us share ourselves, not just with you, but with our wives, husbands, children, and neighbors. You said, 'My grace is sufficient. My strength is made perfect in your weakness. I'll help you. Lo I am with you always, to the end of the earth, and you shall never go alone. You'll never go alone. I'll go with you!' You can boldly say, 'The Lord is my helper!' God will help you do whatever he commands you to do. God will help you do whatever he sends you to do. But God will never accept any excuse for you not doing it. God will say, 'You could have done it, and you should have done it. I commanded you to do it.' You can't come up with some old excuse. 'Well, Lord, I didn't know how, and I don't have any experience.' The Lord said, 'I promised you I would be your helper. We were going to do it together, but you failed on your part of the deal. Now, I must punish you because I was going to help you, but you wouldn't help me. The deal went dead because I had no one to do the job.'

"Lift your hands and say, 'Lord, help me. If there's someone you want to save, someone you want to reach, help me not to fail in doing my part.' The Lord has asked some of you to share, and you've said, 'Lord, I'm not going to talk to that person. I'm not going to share with that person.'

"The Lord will say, 'Give him this, and give him that.'

"Then you'll say, 'Lord, I'm not giving him that because that's mine. I bought it, and I worked for it.'

And the Lord will say, 'Listen, don't you understand I'm trying to do something greater than your possessions. Give it to him. That's the only way I can reach him. Share it!'

"God, I pray in Jesus's name for every mother here. I pray for their strength and courage. I've said some hard things. I know they're hard. I would not have said them, but, Lord, you told me I must say these things. They've got to be said. They must be said. You said, 'That's the reason why I've got you here. Say it! I've made provisions for you. The only reason you don't do it is because you don't want to. You won't will yourself to do it.'

"Now, God, help them accept what has been said. Not to murmur, not to complain, not to get angry, not to make excuses, not to use any alibis but say, 'Lord, help me! Help me! You've said I've got to do it, and I've willed myself to do it! I'm asking for all the strength and all the courage of God to do the job that must be done.'"

How You Can Be Delivered

"Come on. Let's stand, and praise the Lord. We have been redeemed. Hallelujah! God, we thank ya. We praise ya tonight that we have been redeemed. Praise God we've been redeemed by the blood of the Lamb. We've been redeemed by the Savior. We've been redeemed by the Son of God. We have been redeemed. We're grateful, Lord. We're thankful. My God, my God, thank you that we have been redeemed. Yeah, thank you that we have been washed in the blood of the Lamb! Thank you that we've been made children of God. My savior and my God, thank you, Lord. Thank you for these five weeks of the outpouring of the Holy Ghost. This is the Lord's doing, marvelous in our eyes, and to Him alone belongs the honor, glory, and credit. For no one but our God could have done this thing these last five weeks. Thank you for the souls, Lord. Saved, sanctified, baptized, filled with the Holy Ghost, healed, and delivered. Glory to God. Thank ya, my Savior! Keep on moving, keeping on working, keep on pouring out your spirit in a supernatural manner we'll never forget.

"I pray, in Jesus's name, bind every devil and demon, wicked spirit, contrary spirit, and argumentative spirit. My God, every religious spirit in the name of Jesus, I command you to loose and leave here and be cast out in the name of Jesus. God, we pray for the conviction of the Holy Ghost. Every sin, habit, wrong thought, action, or deed that we're guilty of, convict us, convert us, and take control over us so that we will be ready when you come back. That sinner, backslider, hypocrite, man, women, boy, or girl who's not right with God, that person who's about to make a serious mistake, arrest them Lord in the name of Jesus Christ our Savior and Lord.

"In Joel 2:28–32: 'And it shall come to pass afterward, that I will pour out my spirit upon all flesh; and your sons and your daughters shall prophesy, your old men shall dream dreams, your young men shall see visions. And also upon the servants and upon the handmaids in those days will I pour out my spirit. And I will shew wonders in the heavens and in the earth, blood, and fire, and pillars of smoke. The sun shall be turned into darkness, and the moon into blood, before the great and the terrible day of the Lord come. And it shall come to pass, that whosoever shall call on the name of the Lord shall be delivered: for in mount Zion and in Jerusalem shall be deliverance, as the Lord hath said, and in the remnant whom the Lord shall call.'

"Romans 10:9–13 reads: 'If thou shall confess with thy mouth the Lord Jesus, and shalt believe in thine heart that God hath raised him from the dead, thou shalt be saved. For with the heart man believeth unto righteousness; and with the mouth confession is made unto salvation. For the scripture saith, "Whosoever believeth on him shall not be ashamed. For there is no difference between the Jew and the Greek: for the same Lord over all is rich unto all that call upon him. For whosoever shall call upon the name of the Lord shall be saved."' This is the message God has put in our hearts about how we can be saved or delivered.

"I've just read a booklet put out by Teen Challenge. It agrees with the sermon I preached the other night that some of you objected to—'Let the Redeemed of the Lord Say So.' In that sermon, the Holy Spirit said, 'You ought to be grateful enough for what God delivered you out of to tell what God delivered you from.' I got a lot of flak on that. I said, 'For one, if you are not ashamed when the devil made you do it, if you will flaunt it in front of the world and the church, why then, when you get saved, are you afraid to stand up and say "Thank God I was an alcoholic, and God delivered me" or "I was a drug addict, and God delivered me?"' I believe if you're ashamed to say it, you dishonor the Lord who saved you. And if you are not careful, you'll find yourself back in that same condition. Somebody said, 'Well, Brother Lawrence, those are not too bad, but what if the girl was a prostitute? Do you think she oughta stand up and say 'I've been a prostitute?'

"Well, she walked the streets out there for days, weeks, months, and years, telling every man who walked by, 'I'm a prostitute!' Now that God has delivered her, you're telling me she shouldn't testify of God's delivering power. Some lady said to me, 'If she says that, then all of these women are going to come down on her, and who's going to want her for a wife?' The man God has for her. That's the man who's going to want her for a wife. If the man finds out later that his wife was once a prostitute, he's going feel cheated because he was not told. The man is going feel you have represented yourself fraudulently. I was reading this booklet, and in this booklet, an alcoholic testified how God delivered him from alcohol. A homosexual testified how God delivered him from homosexuality. A lesbian testified how God delivered her from lesbianism, and a drug addict was delivered from drug addiction. My heart was blessed when I read of what the grace of God had done in their lives. I don't think any less of them because of what God delivered them from. A child of God is a child of God! Whether you are delivered from a little sin or the greatest of sin, it's a demonstration of the *power* of God.

"The Holy Ghost spoke to my heart and said, 'I want you to preach about how you can be delivered because there are some people out there, bound by those sins, and they don't know how to be delivered. Nobody is telling them they can be delivered. In fact, some people are telling them, "Honey, I'm sorry for you. You'll never be right. You'll never be whole. You have gone so far. Forget it!"'

"Well, that's a lie from hell! God can deliver you from any sin, habit, or wrong the devil can think of! Whosoever shall come to the Lord shall be delivered. If you want deliverance, you got to get past the preacher because he doesn't have it. You got to get past the church because they don't have it. You've got to get to Christ! For Jesus Christ is the deliverer! You've got to come to Him. Some people never get past the preacher. You've got to come to the Lord. The

Lord may send us to stand before you, lay hands on you, or pray for you, but you've got to come all the way to the Lord and come with all your heart.

"It tickles me when some people come up and say they want to be saved, but I can tell they don't really want to be saved. I can sense they think they're doing me a favor by coming up and getting saved. You're not doing me no favor by getting saved. I've been saved. I'm going to stay saved. Now if you ain't got enough sense to get saved, you're going to spend eternity in hell screaming and hollering and calling yourself a fool.

"You must come to the Lord. First, you gotta come humbly. Some folks come struttin' up to the Lord like they're doing him a favor. Listen, you're not doing God a favor! God is doing *you* a favor! You're the sinner, the wretch, the rebellious, and you are the one under a sentence of death. It is God who's delivering you, and you ought to come to him humbly! Some folks will say, 'Well, Brother Lawrence, you don't know who I am.' Well, who are you? 'My name was in big lights on Broadway.' There are whole lot of bums out in the streets whose names were in lights. 'Oh, I've had millions of dollars.' That doesn't make you special because you had money. There are people who've got money, and they aren't fit to live with. In spite of their fame and fortune, they're not fit to live with. You got come to the Lord humbly and sincerely.

"Some people come up to me to get prayed for, and I know they're not sincere. I am not going to use up all my energy on someone who isn't sincere to begin with. From now on, when you come up here for prayer and you're not sincere, I'm going to tell you to pass on. Just pass on. Some of you come up and say, 'Brother Lawrence, pray for me.' Then the Holy Spirit will say to me, 'She's living with a man.' Then I'll say to her, 'What about that man you're living with?' She'll say, 'Well, I don't want you dealing with that.'

"Well I'm not going to pray for you and bless you in your sins! To bless you in your sins damns you. You've got to give up your sins, quit your sins, stop your sins, and get out of your sins. If you don't, you will never have God's blessings. That is the truth. It's a shame a lot of us preachers are hoodwinking the people. We know God will never bless them in their sins, yet we will say a prayer before them, asking God to bless them in their sins. The people need to get right, but the preacher will pray for them anyway because he wants their money. He will bless you, and he knows you're going to hell. But I'm going to tell you the truth so you will never point at me in eternity and say, 'Had you warned me, I could have been saved.' Whoever comes before the Lord humbly and sincerely can be fully delivered.

"God can deliver you—no ifs, ands, buts, or maybes. If you will come to Him, you will be delivered. For some of you, someone had to drag or push you to come like an old mule. An old mule, you'll push him, and he'll just sit down. He won't go anywhere. You'll have to build a fire underneath him to get him up. God is going to build a fire underneath you, but it's going to be too late. The fire will be all around you and all over you. This may be your last chance to get right with God—your last opportunity. God is moving now! Don't talk about next time, later on, or after a while. If you need to get saved, you get saved now! No one knows what's going to happen!

"For whosoever shall call upon the name of the Lord shall be saved. This is what makes me angry. People will come to the altar and won't even open their mouths. The altar worker will lead them in the sinner's prayer, but the mouth of the sinner is completely shut. 'Ask God to forgive you.' They won't open their mouths. So what happens is the altar worker is doing all the praying, and the sinner is saying nothing. You altar workers are not supposed to do all the praying. Make that sinner open his or her mouth and call on God. And if they don't open their mouths, don't tell me they accepted the Lord as their Savior. They haven't accepted anything! 'Well, he accepted the Lord.' How do you know he accepted the Lord? 'He bowed his head.' Uh, open your mouth, and say it! The Bible says, 'Let the redeemed of the Lord say so.' If you've been redeemed, say it! If you can't say it, I don't believe it, and God doesn't either. You've got to call on Him with your mouth. 'Well, I said it in my heart.' No, open your mouth, and confess Him as Lord and Savior of your life!

"Whenever you get folks who won't open their mouths, there's no need to waste a lot of time with them. Just say a little prayer with them, and tell them you hope they will get to the place where they will confess the Lord into their life. You cannot be saved unless you call on the name of the Lord, and his name is Jesus. If you don't call on Him, you're not saved. You're not saved! 'Well, the preacher prayed for me.' That doesn't save you. No preacher praying for you can save you. You have to earnestly pray along with him to receive salvation.

"In Romans 10:9–10 it says, 'That if thou shalt confess with thy mouth the Lord Jesus, and shalt believe in thine heart that God hath raised him from the dead, thou shalt be saved. For with the heart man believeth unto righteousness, and with the mouth confession is made unto salvation.' If you say that you will not confess Him nor call on Him, then you will never be saved. Some people have asked, 'Well, what about little children, they may not know what to say or how to say it?' God may have a special dispensation with children. I don't. It's God's business. All I know is when my children were old enough to understand, I began teaching them how to pray, how to call on the Lord, and how to be saved.

"God said you've got to open your mouth and call on him with your heart. I don't believe any man can come up here to the altar and call on God with all their mind, heart, and spirit and not get an answer from him. I don't believe it! You may come up here and just start repeating the same words over and over again, but your heart was never in it. I remember when the saints were tarrying with me. I just kept saying, 'Jesus, Jesus, Jesus, Jesus, Je-Je-Je-Je-Jesus, Jesus, Jesus, Jesus' while the person was tarrying with me. I would be so happy when they started to slow down because I knew it would soon be over. My heart wasn't in it at all. While they were tarrying with me, I was thinking about walking my girlfriend home. I was never going to get anything from God! Once I made up my mind that I'm going up to the altar, I'm going to forget about everybody. I'm going to call on God with all my heart, with all my mind, and all my spirit. In fifteen minutes, God had baptized me with the Holy Ghost! The

Holy Ghost is telling me your hearts are not in it, and that's why you're not being filled with the Holy Ghost.

"Your heart is not close to God, and I challenge you to come to the altar and say, 'God, I am going to cry out to you with all my heart.' I guarantee you that before the night is over, you'll be speaking in tongues, prophesying, and shouting in the Spirit.

"Your spirit has to be involved in this thing. When your spirit and your heart gets into this thing, nobody can stop you. They'll try to close the service, and you're still speaking in tongues and prophesying. They can pick you up and carry you to the car, and you're still saying, 'Thank you, Jesus. Thank you, Jesus. Thank you, Jesus. Thank you, Jesus!' Listen, when your heart and spirit is involved in seeking God, no one can shut you up. Nobody can shut you up! Isaiah said, 'It was like fire shut up in my bones, and I couldn't forebear. I had to say something about it!'

"If you want to be delivered tonight, God will deliver you. God will save you! God will break the bonds and cords of your desire, feelings and yearnings, and lust and cravings. In each of these testimonies I read, each person said they had to get so caught up in the Word until they no longer listened to their feelings and their emotions. Your emotions will carry you to hell. They will tell you, you can't quit smoking, you've got to keep drinking, you gotta have that man, you gotta have that woman, and you've got to go into that perversion of homosexuality and lesbianism. You tell those emotions, 'No, I'm not going to do it!' You get into God's Word and call on God with all your heart. God will deliver you!"

Deliverance from Sin—Closing Prayer

"There is someone here tonight, and Satan has you totally bound. You are a slave to his desire and to sin. The Holy Spirit said if you would confess you are bound by Satan and that you are helpless in yourself, God will deliver you tonight. God will deliver you tonight, or you can hide, be ashamed to confess it, continue in your sins, and never be delivered. Never!

"The Bible says, 'He that covers his sin shall not prosper.' You'll never get anywhere with God. 'Whosoever confesses and forsaketh shall have mercy.' If you're willing to come and confess and ask God for a deliverance, he will give you a deliverance tonight. It doesn't matter what it is or how long you've been doing this—none of this matters to God. What God is saying is if you hide it, you'll be a slave to it for the rest of your life, and you'll die and go to hell, trying to hide that you're a slave to sin.

"You may say to me, 'I don't want my friends to know. I don't want my family to know.' God will never deliver anybody who continues to hide their sin. He will deliver those who confess and forsake their sins. To them He will bring a deliverance. You are here tonight, in this congregation, and God is dealing with you. God gives you a chance tonight; you can take it and be delivered, and God will bless you. He can make you a blessing, or you can keep on hiding and you'll die and go to hell.

"Bow your heads with me please. Holy Ghost, we ask that you will walk through this audience, lay your hands on the person or persons you're speaking to, and let them confess, 'Lord, I confess that I'm a sinner. I confess this habit of sin and lust, and I confess that I'm bound by Satan with drugs, alcohol, and perversion. I confess, I confess, I confess because, God, tonight I want a deliverance. I don't want to live this kind of life for another minute, another hour, another year, or another day! I want to be delivered, and you're the only one who can deliver me. I need to be delivered, I want to be delivered, and tonight, I'm going to be delivered.'

"God is walking up and down these aisles tonight, saying, 'I'll deliver you! I've delivered others, and I'll deliver you. I've set others free who were bound by the same habit, the same sin, the same lust, and I'll set you free, but you've got to confess it tonight. You've got to own up to it tonight. You must admit it! Then I will bring a deliverance tonight.'

"Work a miracle here tonight. Holy Ghost, have your way. We bind every other spirit. We bind every other force. We bind everything that's not of God in the name of Jesus! We ask that the blood of Jesus Christ come against the enemy, frustrating his power, breaking his hold, and destroying his authority. We ask in the name of Jesus that God would lift up a standard against the enemy tonight, defeat the enemy, and destroy the works of the devil wherever he is, however he is operating in here tonight. Destroy his works, defeat his purpose, and bring to naught all of the lies and all of the workings of Satan because we ask it in Jesus Christ's name. I believe You are here, I believe You will deliver, and I believe you will set free those who would obey you tonight."

Let Jesus Christ Make You a Winner

"In Luke 9:23–26: 'And He said unto them all, "if any man will come after me, let him deny himself and take up his cross daily and follow me. For whoever will save his life, shall lose it. But whosoever will lose his life for my sake, the same shall save it. For what is a man's advantage, if he gain the whole world, and lose himself, or be cast away? For whosoever shall be ashamed of me and of my words, of him shall the son of man be ashamed when he shall come in his own glory, and in his Father's, and of the holy angels."'

"Jesus Christ can make you a winner. Without Jesus Christ, you have already lost everything. Every person without Christ is a loser. 'Well, John Lawrence, he's a rich man.' He's a rich loser! 'He's a famous man.' He's a famous loser! I saw a man with a truck yesterday, and on outside of his truck, he had painted the words, 'A failure in life.' I thought about it and thought it was sad he had come to that conclusion so early on in life and made it into a slogan. But in truth, every man, woman, boy, and girl without Christ is a failure in life. If your life is not lived according to God's plan and his Word, you are a failure. You can lie, cheat, steal, and get a whole lot of stuff, but in God's eyes, you are a failure.

"I heard a story of a man who had two mental breakdowns. He tried to commit suicide. He had been a failure in life until he got converted. Christ came into his life and gave him power and purpose and made him a success in the world. I thought about that, and I said, 'Lord, help me realize and make others realize no matter what is gained in life, without Christ you're a failure and a loser. 'Don't tell me that. I know I'm a success.' A success at what? You own some junk, but in the sight of God, you are a failure in life.

"It takes three things to be a success in life. First of all, it takes the power of God in your life to change you from a sinner into a child of God. I don't care if you're a rebel or an outlaw. It takes the power of God to change you. Without the power of God in your life, you're a loser!

"It takes the presence of God. You know what God said to me today? He said, 'Listen, when I created man, I created him so he and I would live life together. God never created man to live independently from him! It wasn't God's intention for man to stand off by himself without having fellowship and faith in Him. Never! God intended that man and God would be partners in life. They were able to handle anything that would come against their partnership.

"As partners with God, man could handle anything that life would bring his way. Now the devil knew this, so he set out to break up the partnership. He also knew if he went directly to man, then man would have rejected him. Therefore, he went indirectly to man through the woman, creating in her a desire for power. By appealing to her appetite, Satan got her and man to sin, breaking up the partnership between man and God. Until Jesus came on to the scene, man was a failure in life. Jesus Christ made it possible for God and man to come back together again, providing the way for him to be successful.

"It takes the presence of God to be successful. You need God's presence because you will come against devils, demons, wicked spirits, and forces of evil and darkness. You cannot fight Satan by yourself. Nobody can! But when the Holy Spirit fills your heart and mind, Satan is no match for you. He's no match for you and the Holy Spirit. That's why I urge every new convert to continue seek God to get filled with the Holy Spirit. 'Well, John Lawrence, I'm saved.'

"That's a good start, honey, but keep going until you get it all. Now, when you get the Holy Ghost that puts power into your life supernaturally! You have power over all the power of the enemy!

The devil can't do nothing with a Holy Ghost–filled man or woman under the control of the Holy Ghost! You are a failure in life without the power of the Holy Ghost. Life will trip you up, knock you down, and run over you like a steam roller, but, brother, when you've got the power of God in your life, you can stand up to life, overcome life, and master it!

"We are God's servants, so we will do whatever he says. He tells us to go or stay. We used to sing a song in Zion Bible Institute:

'Who am I, that I should chose my way.
The Lord will chose for me.
It's better for, you see.
So let Him bid me, go or stay.'

"If you say, 'Lord, what will you have me do? Give me direction.' God will give you direction, and you won't have any trouble at all. Give your loyalty to Jesus Christ, and let him be the Lord of your life. Jesus Christ will teach you the purpose of God. The majority of mankind don't know where they come from, who they are, and where they're going. That's why they get drunk, take drugs, and jump out of windows. They don't know! But when you come to Jesus Christ, he'll tell you where you came from, who you are, and where you're going! He'll put purpose in your life.

"I feel sorry for drunkards. I feel sorry for them because they have to get drunk in order to face life. They can't face life without their alcohol. Sometimes when I'm up early in the morning, I see them lined up outside the liquor store. They can't face any day without their alcohol. I just look up and say, 'Thank you, Jesus.' I don't need alcohol to face the day or to face life! I've got the power of the Holy Spirit and the presence of God! You're a failure if you don't have Christ in your life.

"'Well, one of these days …'" Some of these brothers really get on my nerves. They're in a fantasy land. 'One of these days, we're goin' to rise up.' You're kidding yourself. All you're going to do is drink yourself to death. They get that stuff in them and start talking crazy. 'We're the real heroes.' What kind of heroes? You won't feed your wife. You won't feed your children. You won't pay the rent. You won't work a lick at a pie factory, and you're talkin' about being a hero? You're in fantasy land.

"Jesus Christ can make you a winner in death. Many folks will do a lot of talking and bragging when they're well, but when they come down with a sickness or a disease or approach the shadow of death, they get afraid. 'I don't know what I'm going to do. I don't want to die.' Well, there aren't many folks who want to die, but we're all going to die. The important thing is being prepared to die. The Christian is the only person prepared to die. When he gave his heart to Jesus Christ and gave up his sins, this prepared him to die. So whether he lives or die, he doesn't have to be afraid. The power of death has been broken by the power of our resurrected Savior, Jesus Christ. When the Christian has finished the work God has given him to do, Jesus will be standing there to welcome him home!

"You need to start making preparations for your eternity. You can get so caught up with this world, this life, getting, possessing, and owning until you forget about making preparations for your eternity. If you're a child of God, if you've been born again, if you've been filled with the spirit and have fulfilled God's purpose for your life, then you're a winner. Christ has made you a winner! You're a winner for all eternity. A person may ask, 'Are you saying there will be losers and winners in eternity?' Yes, I am. The winners are those who are going to be crowned and rule and reign with Christ. The losers are those who are to be bound, hand and foot, and cast into hell, into outer darkness! Throughout all eternity, they're going to weep, grit their teeth, curse and swear. In vain, they will plead and pray.

"It is not God's will for anyone to go to hell. God doesn't want a single soul to perish! God doesn't want a single soul to be lost! Hell was created for the devil and his angels. You go to hell because you climbed over God's mercy and grace. You go to hell because you climb over God's Son, the Holy Ghost, and the gospel of Jesus Christ. You go to hell against God's will! You get that!"

Backsliders: Opening Prayer

" Come on, and let's praise the Lord for this miracle of you being here tonight. Hallelujah, thank you, Lord! A miracle of God. My God, in Jesus's name, we thank ya, we praise ya, we glorify ya, and we exalt ya because there's no God like you in the whole universe! Thank you, Lord, for loving us and creating us in your own image. Thank you, Lord, for loving us and sending Jesus Christ. Hallelujah! Thank you, Lord, for loving us and saving us out of our sins from demons and devils and powers of darkness. Thank you, Lord, for filling us with the Holy Ghost. Thank you, Lord, for inviting us to spend all of eternity with you in heaven. We thank you today. We pray your blessing over every person coming into the service tonight. God bless all who are here tonight. Touch all, encourage all, speak to all, heal all, and whatever the needs are. God meet the needs! Do a miracle of God for those who are troubled, burdened, and disturbed. God, in the name of Jesus Christ, the Son of God, work a miracle here tonight. Break the heart of that sinner and those backsliders tonight. God, you love the backslider. God, you are calling for the backslider. Hallelujah! God, you are married to the backslider! All the backsliders need to do is come back to you, be restored, and be renewed in the name of Jesus Christ, the son of the living God. Send your word like a mighty hammer, and let it break into pieces. Like a sharp sword, let it cut asunder. Like a mighty fire, let it consume everything unlike God and his Christ in Jesus's mighty name!

"Well, this is a miracle of God. I tried my best, and I prayed so hard that it wouldn't snow, but it snowed anyhow. Now the only other prayer I could pray is, 'Lord, send the saints out, make them come out, command them to come out,' and you are here. I thank God for you. I certainly want to thank everyone who pressed their way out over adverse conditions to be here tonight. God has a blessing for you tonight. God has a blessing for you! Because of your faithfulness and perseverance, you have to really love the Lord to come out on a night like tonight. God has done so much for us, and we ought to do all we can for the Lord! I want to thank Bishop Caesar for extending the revival. You are blessed and privileged here at Bethel to have a man of God who loves God. I can't say that about every preacher.

"Some preachers don't say nothing. They don't love God! They don't care what God wants. They don't care what God's will is. They do what they want to do! I went to one preacher's church, and the Lord told me to pray for the sick. I made the announcement that I was going to pray for the sick. He got up and said he wasn't going to let Elder Lawrence pray for the sick. There was nothing I could do. He was the pastor of the church, and I didn't pray for the sick. But I said to the Lord, "Get me out of here as quick as you can!" That guy was crazy! I went to the church to train them for soul winning, and I trained them for soul winning. He said to me, "Brother Lawrence, don't be surprised that if tomorrow, there will be no one there but you and I." I said, "I would be surprised." When tomorrow came, there were eighty people standing outside, waiting to go out to knock on doors and witness to the people in that community. He was surprised. If you give people what God told you to give them, God will bless people and make them a blessing! You have a man here who loves God, and he loves people! I know a lot preachers who don't love God, and I know some who loves God but don't love people. They will sit and talk about people like a dog, and it grieves my spirit to be around them. I don't believe you should talk about God's people because God's people are the finest people in the world! Can you say Amen? There are no finer people in the world than the people of God! God says that about his own children.

"Turn with me to the Word of the Lord found in the Book of John 6:59–63: 'These things said He in the synagogue as He taught in Capernaum. Many of his disciples, when they had heard this, said, This is an hard saying; who can hear it? When Jesus knew in himself that his disciples murmured at it, he said unto them, 'Doth this offend you? What if you see the Son of man ascend up where he was before? It is the spirit that quicketh; the flesh profiteth noting.'

"All that the flesh does and accomplishes outside of God is worth nothing. The flesh profiteth nothing! For the moment, it looks important. For the moment, it looks grand! However, in the next moment, it's gone. All of your bragging and boasting profits nothing. It's here one moment, gone the next moment, and forgotten! Every sinner, backslider, and hypocrite ought to remember that Jesus says, 'The words that I speak unto you, they are spirit, and they are life' (John 6:63). God's Word and God's spirit are the eternal things. The things you do in the flesh outside of God, means nothing. Do you know how long it takes your flesh to rot? God takes his breath and spirit from you, and in four days, you start to rot. In four days, it begins to rot, and your flesh turns back into dust.

"I spoke to a person recently who was very close to me. I performed the wedding ceremony for his daughter. I spoke to him about the Lord, and he wasn't ready to hear it and wouldn't receive it. He sat down at his dining room table and called his wife he was separated from. He had left his wife and his children and was living in a house by himself. The devil will make a fool out you. That's why I'm telling you girls all these fellas who ask you about marrying them, don't marry nobody until you check with the Lord. Don't marry nobody until you check with your mama. Say, 'Mama, what do you think about this boy?' If mama looks him over and say 'Nothing from nothing leaves nothing, and that ain't nothing,' then run for your life! She knows more about men than you know! Ask your dad about him. If he says 'Nothing from nothing leaves nothing, and that ain't nothing,' don't even waste any time with him because that nothing will reduce you to nothing! Do you hear me? If a fellow or girl ain't nothing, then you will be nothing!

"God is talking to someone here tonight. You're about get yourself into a mess that you will never get out of. Never! 'Well, I'll leave him.' You ain't out of it because you leave him. A bum will follow you to the end of the earth. 'I'll get a divorce.' Some of these fellas don't care about a divorce! He'll come and blow your brains out with your divorce papers in your hand! Divorce doesn't mean nothing to some of these crazy folks! You see it in the papers. Just the other day, a woman got a divorce and left the man. He came to the job, waited for her, and killed her and the man she was interested in. Don't even get tied up with those kind of folks. When you pray and ask God, and God will say nothing! That means there's nothing to him, and don't even consider it! Say 'Hi and goodbye.' To some folks, that's all you need to say—'Hi and bye.' Y'all lookin' real funny here tonight. God's talking to you! You're about to get your life tied up with somebody. You'll never get away from! Not ever! Not until you're dead and in your grave! If you're not careful, they will make you lose what you have in God, and you'll go to hell with him. And that's terrible! Even in hell, you got to look at him and say, 'Lord, that's the reason I'm here.' I'm not joking tonight. You better listen. You better listen! I'm serious! I was trying to make another point, and the Holy Ghost said, 'No, stop here, and warn somebody. Warn somebody!'

"You may say to yourself, 'But he looks so handsome.' That doesn't mean a thing! 'She's so cute looking.' What's in the person! When folks who got the devil in them, there ain't nothing to them. God is warning somebody here tonight! You're about to make that decision, and God is saying 'Don't do it!' God is telling you to wait until you get someone worth marrying. 'Well, he's a man.' Maybe, but everything you see don't have to be a man! My wife and I sometimes see someone, and we both wonder. I know it's not a man. Is it a woman? My wife will say, 'I don't know.' Only God can deal with something like that. You better know what you're doing! Ask God, your parents, and the man or woman of God. You know, some of you don't even know about speaking to God. Some of y'all don't even speak to God, and he doesn't speak to you! I see you come up here night after night, and in two minutes, you're right back to your seat. You're not talking to God.

"The other night, the Holy Ghost said to a young girl, 'Give that ring back!' Later on, a girl came up to me and said, 'I got a ring, but the Lord wasn't talking to me.' She had hidden the ring from her mother and father. Listen, if you've got to hide the ring, something is wrong with the whole deal! The engagement ring ought to be the proudest thing you have, and you should be showing it to everybody. If there's something wrong with the deal in the beginning, it's going to be a mess at the end! God is warning someone here tonight. Ask the man or woman of God. The devil has got your brain like mush. You don't know what's right or wrong or up or down. So don't go by your brain. Ask the man or woman of God. Let them pray with you, and let them tell you what doth saith the Lord! 'Well, they will say don't marry him.' If they say don't marry him, if you ever want to be happy, don't marry them. 'Well, what do they know?' When they have talked with God, they know the mind of God. 'Well, they don't know Johnny.' They don't have to know Johnny. They know the God who made Johnny, and if God says no, then don't marry him. If you ever want any happiness, don't marry him. For just as sure as your parents and God told you not to marry him, if you go ahead and marry him, you're going to catch hell for as long as you live! If God tells you not to put your life with that person's life, you listen to God! Listen to God! If you defy God, you will never be happy. The relationship will never work. There will never be any peace. There will never be any joy. There will never be any happiness because God told you in the beginning not to do it! God is warning you for the last time about this relationship. It is not of God, it will never be of God, and it will always be a tragedy in your life! If you walk over God's reproof and God's counsel, you will suffer until the day you die.

"Thank you, Lord Jesus. Thank ya for dealing with us and speaking to us, trying to save us from heartbreak, heartache, and tragedy. Thank ya! You're a mighty God, a great Savior, and a mighty deliverer, and we thank you tonight because there's no one like you in this whole universe.

"I was talking about this man who left his wife. His wife called him and said, 'I need more money.'

"He said, 'Tell that woman to shut up!'

"She said, 'I don't have enough money for the children.'

"He said, 'Tell that woman I don't want to even hear her voice!' He said a few more things and hung up the phone. He had a heart attack and died, sitting in that chair. The last thing he said to his wife, the mother of his eight children, was 'Shut up. I don't want to hear your voice.'

"Now you can jump outta here if you want to and act like a fool when your minister, parents, and friends are telling you not to do it. You've got to be crazy. That man died telling his wife to shut up, and he didn't want to hear her voice. It was four days before they discovered that man's body. They smelled a bad odor. Finally, they broke down the door and found him sitting there rotting, decaying in his chair. This man, four days earlier, was a big black proud good-looking man. Now, four days later, he was rotten and stinking. So don't tell me about your flesh! Jesus said it profits nothing, and outside the will of God, it ain't good for nothing! Your flesh, contrary to the will of God, ain't good for nothing! You better understand that. Jesus said his words are life. They're spirit. Accept them, you'll live and you become spirit. Reject them, you die and you become dirt! It's up to you! Lift your hand and say, 'Lord keep on speaking to me.'

"'For Jesus knew from the beginning who they were that believed not, and who should betray him. From that time many of his disciples went back, and walked no more with him' (John 6:64, 66). This is a description of a backslider. A person who walked with God, talked with God, and fellowshipped with God, but because something happened in their life and in their relationship, they decided, 'I can't take it, I'm not going to make it, and I'm not going to walk with God anymore. I'm going back to the world, my sins, my friends, my family, and wherever I was before I started walking with God.' Oh you may still come to church, but you have already backslidden.

"When you see the saints, you say, 'I'm all right. The Lord knows. I may not come to church anymore, but God and I have a good time in my house.' The Bible says, 'Not forsaking the assembling of yourselves together, as the manner of some is; but exhorting one another: and so much the more, as ye see the day approaching.' God doesn't want folks staying at home. God wants his people to come together, encouraging one another, fellowshipping with one another, blessing one another, and praying for one another. That's the only way you're going to keep moving on in Christ. Proverbs 14:12, 14 deals graphically with the backslider: 'There is a way which seemeth right unto a man, but the end thereof are the ways of death. The backslider in heart shall be filled with his own ways.'

"When you get to the point where no one can tell you what is right, what is wrong, and what to do, no one can control you, you know more than preacher, you know more than the teacher, and you know more than anybody, you're on your way to becoming a backslider. The Lord told me backsliding first begins in the mind. When you're saved, God holds your attention. When you backslide, you take your attention from God and put it on something else. Sometimes a good Christian is living for the Lord and loving the Lord, and all of a sudden, the devil sends a person, an event, or something that grabs their attention. Instead of keeping your mind on the Lord, you start placing your attention on an ambition, goals, or person. Now you haven't committed an act or deed of a backslider yet, but you've already begun to backslide. You cannot give the world, flesh, the devil, or other persons your attention and stay with the Lord. The Lord should always have your full attention. Your mind should always be on the Lord. The Bible says, 'Thou wilt keep him in perfect peace, whose mind is stayed on thee: because he trusteth in thee" (Isa. 26:3). Stay riveted on the Lord! Keep your mind stayed on Him. The Bible tells us to think on the things that are true, honest, just, pure, lovely, of good report, any virtue, and any praise.

"The backslider allows his attention to wander away from the Lord to other things, and as he continues down that path, his very affection is taken from the Lord and given to somebody else. I see so many of our young folks get saved. Their attention and affection is centered on God, but then the devil sends some handsome or cute little somebody. All of sudden, they take their whole attention off the Lord and places it on this person, saying, 'It must be love!' Sometimes the girl or boy are not even thinking about you! I've heard of girls who are a few months away from finishing college, drop out, talking about how 'they're in love' and want to get married. You must be crazy! Finish your education and your training because you're going to need it in this life. 'Well, he said he can't wait.' Tell him to go, and take a cold shower! Go and run around the track a few times! There's no such thing as 'you can't wait.' You've been waiting this long. 'Well, he said "either marry me, or get somebody else."' When a man tells you that, tell him to get somebody else! When a man wants you, he doesn't want anyone else! So tell him to go ahead because if you want somebody else, then you don't want me, and if you want somebody else, I don't want you! I want somebody to want me and only me!

"Let me warn you, don't give your heart to no one but the Lord and to whoever the Lord chooses for you to give your love to. If you give your heart to people God didn't tell you to give it to, they will break it and hand it back to you. Who is worthy of taking your love and affection from God? I will never take my love for God and give it to anybody. The love I give to God belongs to him. When you take all your love and give it to a human being, you're headed for disaster! Don't give your heart to someone who's going to tear it to pieces! You better listen to God. People will fail you, but God will never fail you! The scripture came to me: 'Nevertheless I have somewhat against thee, because thou hast left thy first love.' Hear what the Lord says, 'You used to be in love with me. I used to be the joy of your life, the light of your life. But someone else has come along, and you have left your first love!' Don't ever leave God, your first love. What a tragic thing for God to say to someone.

"The backslider, in heart, is filled with his own ways. He doesn't care about God, and he doesn't respond to God. He'll say, 'Oh, I get tired of going to church. I get tired of listening to those preachers. I get tired of reading the Bible. I get tired of praying.' He's tired of all the things of God. The going to discos, the drinking, the smoking of joints, all the other stuff, he'll say, 'Now this really living. Living!'

If that's all the living you've got, then five minutes from now, you can be dead, reaching for hell, with no hope for the future. Lift your hands and say, 'Lord, have mercy.'

"Up to this point, you haven't broken your loyalty to God. Your love toward Him might have cooled off, but there's still a certain kind of loyalty to God. The devil is persuasive and smooth, and he'll keep talking and talking until you get to a low period in your walk. He'll say, 'You've given me your mind, your affections, and you've cooled off toward God. Now I want all of you. To prove it, I want you to do this deed and commit this act.' You have to decide to keep your contract with God or break it. You've got to watch your low periods. Everyone has a low period. It could be a certain time of year, or month, week, or day. It could last for weeks or even months. Be careful not to make any decisions during those times.

"The words of Paul comes to me, and he said, 'Demas has forsaken me, having loved this present world.' There comes a time when you have to make up your mind to either be loyal to God, or be with the world. If you go with the world, your very soul pulls itself away from God, and you go out into sin! You go out into darkness away from Jesus, the light of world. When Judas made up his mind to betray the Lord and he walked outside, it was dark naturally and even darker spiritually! Jesus said, 'I am the light of the world!' When Judas turned his back on the light of the world, he never saw light anymore, only darkness!'

"'Well, Brother Lawrence, I've backslidden. What must I do?' The first thing is to renounce the sin or the person that caused you to backslide! 'Well, I don't want to hurt their feelings.' You're worried about hurting their feelings when you should be concerned about going to hell and the feelings you're going to have while burning in hell! Forget their feelings! Tell them, 'I'm not going to be a barbecue for you!' It may sound funny to them, but let them laugh. You must renounce them and let them laugh all the way to hell! Renounce the person. Renounce the sin. Renounce whatever it was that caused you to backslide. The feelings, the emotions, renounce it! You'll never be free until you renounce it. I don't mean apologize to him or her. I remember the story of one woman who was going with a man. They were shacking up together. He was caught committing a crime and went to jail. While he was in jail, she got saved. So he kept saying, 'When I get out, were going to get back together again.'

"She came to me and said, 'Brother Lawrence, I don't know what I'm going to do. This man is coming out. I used to live with him, and I know if I don't live with him, he'll kill me. He told me he would kill me, and this man would do it!'

"'Come on, let's pray,' I said. 'Lord, I bind this devil and rebuke this devil in the name of Jesus. I command, Lord, that he'll leave this woman alone.'

"He came out of jail, went to her, and said, 'You live with me or I'm going to kill you.' She just prayed. He saw she had changed and was different. She gave him her testimony. Once she finished testifying, he looked at her and said, 'Well, if that's the way it is, goodbye.' And he left her! Renounce the person, renounce the sin, and renounce the relationship. Renounce the spirit. Some of you are caught up by evil spirits. That takes the place of human beings in your life.

"Remove the cause. If you were shacking with someone, come and get saved. Become unshackled! Either they go, or you go! 'Well, I'm going to go and sleep on the sofa.' That ain't goin' to work. Get out the house, and leave the premises! If a person made you backslide, you can't hang around them and front slide! You've got to get away from that person. If they were paying the rent, then you got go get a job and pay your own rent! If you belonged to some kind of cult or group, once you get saved, you've got to come out of it. You tell them, 'Listen, I want you all to know where I stand from now on out. I'm a child of God. I'm saved, and what I've been doing, I'm not going to do anymore.'

"They may say, 'Well, if that's the way it is, you can't be a part of us.'

"You reply, 'Well, as of this moment, I'm not a part of you.' Nicki Cruz had given up the gang once he got saved. Tom Skinner had to give up the gang once he got saved. They were leaders of gangs. You cannot get right with God holding on to sin or sinners. You gotta to give it up! Remove the cause, or remove yourself. Sometimes you have to leave your own family. Many Christians had to leave home and their families. In some cultures, when you leave the family for Jesus, the family will hold funerals and pronounce you dead. If they see you in the streets, they won't even acknowledge you. If they see you hungry, they wouldn't give you a piece of bread. If you will say, 'Lord, I'm giving myself to you. I'll give up my family, and I'll give up my friends. I'll give up anything, but I will never give You up!' God will stand with you, and God will bless you!

"Backslider, if you want to come back to God, renew your faith and your fellowship with the Lord Jesus Christ. You can't stay out there with those folks and hang with them. You can't agree with them and keep faith and fellowship with Jesus Christ. 'But, Brother Lawrence, I'm trying to win them.' You can't win them by agreeing with them. No, no! No one else has been able to do it, and you won't be able to do it. They got to agree with you if you're going to win them. If you agree with them, you'll sink to their level, and you'll end up back in your sins. You have to come out of your sins and say to them, 'From here on, I agree with the Word of God, and I agree with Jesus the Son of God. He's my savior, and He's my Lord!' There are a whole lot of people who say Jesus is the white man's God. Many people have challenged me on that. They have said, 'Didn't you know the black people's God is Allah?' Then I saw the movie *Roots*, and that poor man called on Allah but Allah never did answer him. Everyone who called on Jesus got delivered. I don't care what color He is. All I know is his name is Jesus, and every time I call on him, he answers. Jesus is everyman's God, and he saved me out of my sins. He gave me a hope and a reason for living, and I will serve Him!

"Renew your faith, and renew your fellowship in the Lord Jesus Christ. I don't care what it cost. 'Brother Lawrence, what if they actually threaten to take my life if I give my life to Jesus. What happens if they actually kill me?' If it means dying, Jesus said, 'If you lose your life for my sake and the gospel's sake, you'll find it again! But if you save your life, you will lose it.'"

Watch Your Mind—Opening Prayer and Dialogue

"Come on. Let's stand, and thank God for being so rich. Father, we thank ya. Hallelujah for all the richness you've given us. Thank you, Lord. We're sons and daughters of the almighty God, and all things are ours, given to us from God, our Father. We're grateful and thankful, Lord, for how rich we are! We just glorify and magnify ya. We exalt you because you alone are worthy of honor, praise, and thanksgiving. Thank you, Lord, for the extra days of this revival. Somebody is still outside, and you want to bring them in before the door is closed. Somebody is still disobedient, and you want them to surrender and become obedient to God before the door is closed. Somebody has not received the gift of the Holy Ghost, and it is time for them to receive the gift of the Holy Ghost. We pray that this very night, they will leave here speaking in tongues, prophesying, and magnifying the name of the Lord. Oh God, fulfill thy purpose and thy plan in our lives so that there will be no regrets once we step on the other side of glory. So that there will be no sad remembrances or moaning for something we left undone.

"Help us to do whatever it is that we ought to do so that we would please you with all of our hearts in the name of Jesus Christ, our Savior and Lord. God bless ya. If you're sick tonight, we want you to come and stand at the altar that we may anoint you for healing! For those of you who have special desires of your heart, we're going to touch and agree with you for God to grant you these desires according to his will and plan for your life. The Bible says, 'That if two of you shall agree on earth as touching anything that they shall ask, it shall be done for them of my Father which is in heaven.' Sometimes you need someone else to pray along with you for the request you have before God. Some may say their faith is strong enough and they don't need anyone to pray with them. There have numerous times when I have prayed, and nothing happened. I would then go to a brother or sister, and ask them to give me their hand and pray with me. Then God would answer my prayer. Don't ask God for something that belongs to someone else. You're not going to get it, and you can forget it! If it belongs to someone else and you want it, that's covetousness, so don't even ask for it!

"In our meeting with the young unmarried people, the women said there weren't no available young men in the church. So we dealt with the topic, 'Men Who Are Interested in You.' We witnessed with them and shared Christ with them. If he's not saved, don't share nothing but Christ with him. That's right! You can't be hugging and kissing a sinner and not get in trouble! So many women get messed up then want to cover up, and it only brings disgrace on you and the church. If a young man is interested in you, lead him to the Lord. Tell him about the Lord! I believe if you work with God, he will work with you! I just believe that with all my heart.

"God had extended these services because somebody prayed. Somebody asked God to extend the service, and God answered your prayer for a threefold purpose!

Purpose #1

"Some of you have unsaved love ones who better get saved now or they will never get saved. I talked to a man about a month or two ago. I was performing the wedding for his daughter. I spoke to him about the Lord and getting saved, and he wasn't ready to get saved. He hoped that someday he'd get ready. About a month later, they found him dead in a room in his house. He had been dead for four days, gone into eternity. God gave him a chance to get saved, and it's too late now. He's in hell screaming for mercy, but there's no mercy to be found. I want to warn any sinner, backslider, hypocrite, and person out of fellowship with God that he has extended this revival to get you right. God said, 'Don't play the fool!' Get yourself right with God! Someone said, 'Well, I'm supposed to be right.' I'm not talking about what you're supposed to be. If you're not right, you're not right. I'm talking about getting yourself right with God!

"Some of you haven't brought one relative to the meeting at all this week. You can witness to them yourself, and you can bring them to the house of the Lord where the servants of God have an opportunity to reach them. Two young ladies walked in here Sunday night after the sermon was preached. They didn't even hear the message. I was making my altar call, and they walked in. One of them said to other, 'Let's go up.' They came right to the altar and surrendered to Christ. Then they went downstairs and got baptized. God can save them if we get them here! God has extended this revival, not because I wanted him to do it but because somebody needs to be saved! After the meeting is over, judgment is going to fall! God has held back the judgment so somebody can make their peace with God.

Purpose #2

"He has also extended this meeting so some of us, who are deliberately disobedient, might yield to the urging of the Holy Ghost! The most dangerous thing to do is to sit in God's house and deliberately disobey the Holy Ghost!

Purpose #3

"Those of you who did not receive the baptism of the Holy Ghost, God wants you to get it! You'll never be the Christian you ought to be, you'll never be a witness for God, and you'll never be used by God as you ought to be until you receive the baptism of the Holy Ghost!

"This is for those of you who have gotten saved during this meeting. If the church you are presently a member of did not preach the gospel to you strong enough for you to get saved, you are to seek the Lord to find out if you should go back to that church or not. I'm going to be honest with you. I believe where God saved you, where the people are concerned about you, and where they work with you to get you through to God, is the place where God wants you to be. So get before God, and ask him what he wants you to do. I highly suspect he's talking to you right now, telling you, 'If this is where I saved you, this is where you should join.' You might be attending where your grandfather, grandmother, mother, and father belongs to. Don't let that be the reason why you're going to stay. Are your parents saved? Is the pastor preaching the full gospel? If the folks at your church are not getting saved, you better run for your life. Many times you'll come out of a situation, and you get saved and then you try to go back into it. However, the folks in it are not saved, and they don't want you to be saved. They certainly don't want you coming back there and condemning them.

"I remember when I was preaching out in Philadelphia, Pennsylvania, and a woman who was an alcoholic heard me preaching on the radio. She came to the service, and told me she wanted to get rid of this alcoholism. I told her to come on down and get saved! God saved her, and made her give up her drinking. When she went back to her church, the folks said to her, 'Well, you don't have to give up your drinking. Come on and drink with us. All of us drink.' They tried to make her give up her salvation, and return to drinking again. Now it was killing that woman. It was destroying her home and her marriage, but they wanted her to come back into that bondage. I told her, 'Listen, honey, God brought you out. You better stay out, stay saved, and get filled with the Holy Ghost!'

"God doesn't save folks just so they go back to do the same things they were doing before they got saved. That's a waste of the grace of God. I can just hear some you speaking to yourself, 'Well, we got a group I belong to, and I've got a position in the church.' You ask your heavenly Father what you should do! I don't care what kind of group you're in or what kind of position you hold in the church. If God says to come out from among them and be ye separated, get out and separate yourself! God knows what he has planned for your future. You don't know! God knows what he's going to do for you and how he's going to bless you, and he will not, and cannot do it if you are disobedient to the voice of the Holy Ghost! You better help me just a little bit here, Lord!

"God shook me up today. I mean, the Lord really shook me up today. Turn to Philippians 2:1–11: 'If there be therefore any consolation in Christ, if any comfort of love, if any fellowship of the spirit, if any bowels and mercies, fulfill ye my joy, that ye be likeminded, having the same love being of one accord, of one mind. Let nothing be done through strife or vainglory; but in lowliness of mind let each esteem other better than themselves. Look not every man on his own things, but every man also on the things of others. Let this mind be in you, which was also in Christ Jesus: Who, being in the form of God, thought it not robbery to be equal with God: But, made himself of no reputation, and took upon him the form of a servant, and was made in the likeness of men: And being found in fashion as a man, he humbled himself, and became obedient unto death, even the death of the cross. Wherefore God also hath highly exalted him, and given him a name which is above every name: That at the name of Jesus every knee should bow, of things in heaven, and things in earth, and things under the earth; And that every tongue should confess that Jesus Christ is Lord, to the glory of God the Father.'

"If you want to know what kind of mind to have, the Bible tells you. I've been thinking, why do so many people backslide? Our backsliding rate is too great. Once you come out of darkness into this light, you should never go back! Not ever! But we do have a high backsliding rate, and I asked God why? People get gloriously saved, some gloriously filled, and yet they don't go far and don't stay long. Some of the reasons are we don't take enough time with them, we don't show enough care for them, and we don't have enough follow up procedures in place. People need to attend the new converts' classes. Get in those classes! You got saved, filled, and you only got a good feeling. The devil can send something your way, and knock that good feeling right out of you. You need the understanding and the knowledge of the scriptures! You need to grow and develop properly, and you can't do it by yourself. Get in those classes, learn, develop, and grow.

"God told me the reason why so many people backslide so quickly is because they do not watch their minds. The Holy Ghost has been saying to me all day, 'Watch your mind!' Many of God's people allow the enemy to dump anything he wants into their minds. You can't stay saved and let the devil put anything he wants to into your mind. God dealt with me about a worldly mind. If you don't watch your mind, the devil will put the things of the world in your mind. In 1 John 2:15–17, the Lord says, 'Love not the world, neither the things that are in the world. If any man love the world, the love of the Father is not in him. For all that is in the world, the lust of the flesh, and the lust of the eyes, and the pride of life, is not of the Father, but is of the world. And the world passeth away, and the lust thereof: but he that doeth the will of God abideth for ever.' If you don't watch your mind, the devil will put lust in your mind.

"I saw the danger of television and the danger of the movies. Now when Bishop Caesar and I and others were coming along, they didn't allow us to go to the movies. They weren't able to give us scripture for this. They just said it was of the devil. You're not supposed to go, and they dared us to go. Because if you went, they'd put you out of the church! There were no ifs or ands. If they heard about you or caught you going to the movies, out! Today we are more lenient, and we don't have any strong saints either! We don't have any spiritual giants. We have a whole lot of lukewarm folks!

"The Lord showed me that through the movies and television, Satan controls your mind. It is lust that he stirs up in your mind. Movies and television shows are normally not geared to help the Christian. There are good Christian programs, but it is generally geared to stir up a lust for things! It will have you wanting everything you see. It kills the appetite for the spiritual. It kills the desire for the spiritual things of God. It creates a lust in you for worldly, carnal, and fleshly things, and it will have you arguing against God. You'll start saying, 'I don't see anything wrong with this or that. I don't see no harm!' God showed me that it creates a lust for the flesh! If you're watching a bedroom scene, one or two things is going to happen. You'll either get disgusted and turn it off or your eyes will get big and you'll get real interested. However, what you don't realize is it is stirring up a lust in you. A lust for the flesh, killing the spiritual, and destroying the godly. If you're not careful, sooner or later, you will leave the spiritual place you were standing, go toward that place of the flesh, and eventually die spiritually.

"God told me to guard your mind because Satan is at war with the people of God to attack us and defeat us through our minds. He doesn't care how long you shout, how much you speak in tongues, or how deep you are. If he can get a hold of your mind, you won't be spiritual very long! 'Let this mind be in you, which was also in Christ Jesus.' That is the only way to stay saved. That's the only way to hold out. That's the only way to hold on. God brought me to the Book of John chapter 8 where Jesus said unto the people, 'You are of your father, the devil, and the lusts of your father you will do. He was a murderer from the beginning, born not in the truth. There's no truth in him because when he speaks a lie, he speaks of his own, for he is a liar, and the father of it.'

"The movies and TV shows are the biggest liars we've ever known, and we believe these lies. We've become a part of these lies. We've become absorbed in these lies, and we don't recognize what Satan is doing. He's stirring up lust, desires, and abnormal, unnatural things. And sooner or later, unless you realize what's going on, you will be defeated in your spiritual life. The first thing you do is that you'll stop praying. Then you'll stop reading the Word and then you stop coming to church. And then it's not long before you're out there doing every ungodly, unholy, and unnatural thing that everybody else is doing. Watch your mind! Watch your mind!

"'Brother Lawrence, I see no harm.' You know, they say you can boil a frog by putting him into warm water and start increasing the temperature a little at a time. Now the stupid frog will sit there and be boiled alive. You see, the temperature increases so slowly that the frog gets adjusted to each increase in temperature, and before long, he's been boiled alive! The devil is pulling that same trick on us! He's increasing the level of immorality and depravity so slowly until you can't distinguish right from wrong or detect when the spirit of God has left you! You'll feel, 'I'm a Christian. I'm a child of God!' You're still testifying, and the spirit of God is gone! Like Samson, we don't even realize that the power of God has departed. We're still quakin', shakin', and hollerin,' but the power of God is gone! Sometimes we are still preaching, and there is no anointing, no authority, no soul, no words! God said, 'Watch your mind! Watch your mind!' The devil will flip things in your mind in such a subtle way that you won't even know it.

"In Mark 4:19, it reads, 'And the cares of this world, and the deceitfulness of riches, and the lusts of other things entering in, choke the word, and it becometh unfruitful.' If you don't watch your mind, the devil will burden you with the cares of this world to the extent that you forget the things you've got to do for God and eternity. The devil will make you get so caught up with the cares, caught up with this life, lusting after things, until you'll let your eternal soul die and go to hell! Watch your mind! Watch your mind. Watch what you read, what you see, and what you're putting in your mind. You don't realize that the homosexuals, lesbians, unrighteous, and unnaturals have said, 'We're going to strip America of all of her morals. We're going to tear down all Christian principles. We're going to make folks accept anybody and anything.'

"The last frontier is incest. Now that homosexual and lesbians agenda has been accepted by the politicians, these same people are now trying to say it is all right for father and daughter to have sex, mother and son to have sex, and brother and sister to have sex. Yes, these same politicians have entered this next frontier of moral depravity. They are doing this right now and trying to make their case so convincing that enough people will say, 'Well, I can see their point.' No, I don't see no point! It's wrong in the sight of God. It's wrong because God said it's wrong. It's unholy, it's unnatural, and it's ungodly, and they're trying to make you accept it! They're making you believe it! They're making you receive it! If you're not careful, they will make you become a part of it! Do you hear me? They'll make you become a part of it!

"They're making thousands of women say, 'We don't want to get married. We just want to live with a man. Marriage is not important, as long as you love each other.' A man who loves a woman wants that woman to be his wife. A woman that loves a man, wants that man to be her husband! Anybody who doesn't want to marry you, doesn't love you! Don't let anybody fool you!

"Watch your mind, watch you mind, watch your mind. I saw that worldly mind, and I saw that mind of lust for the things that makes us proud. The church is almost getting to the place where we have become the proudest people you can find. God's people should not be proud, but rather humble. The devil will make you proud of who you are, what you've got, and proud of what you think you're going to get. We have the right to be grateful and thankful, but never a right to be proud! Whatever we got, God gave it to us, and what the Lord giveth, the Lord can take away! Blessed be the name of the Lord!

"Watch your mind! Don't allow anything to put lust, desire, or pride in you. All of these things are going to pass away. Only they who do the will of God is going to abide forever. Romans 12:1 really thrilled my heart. Listen to what it says: 'I beseech you therefore, brethren, by the mercies of God, that ye present your bodies a living sacrifice, holy, acceptable unto God, which is your reasonable service. And be not conformed to this world: but be ye transformed by the renewing of your mind, that ye may prove what is that good, and acceptable, and perfect will of God.'

"Be not conformed to this world. Don't let the world shape you. You shape the world. Don't let the world pour you into its mold and you become an exact replica of the world. Rather, resist the world, fight it, and oppose it. Today, we don't oppose the world. We don't fight the world. We join them. We have become a part of the world. The world can come in, sit in our services, and feel quite comfortable. The world can sit in our pulpits and feel comfortable. The world can get up and preach to us, and we feel good as the world ministers to us. But I can remember the day when the world was afraid to walk into a sanctified church because the *power* of the Holy Ghost would knock them on the floor, and they would leave running. As far as coming up to the altar or the pulpit, they dare not come up to the altar. There was power at the altar, and no preacher who wasn't living right wouldn't dare come up to the pulpit to preach. Some of those good old Holy Ghost–filled folks would start speaking in tongues, like thunder, and would scare them half to death. Nowadays, we got the people with the gifts of the spirit scared to even say a word! God is going to judge us just as sure as we live.

"Watch your mind, and don't let the world conform you to their standards. Don't let the world decide what you should and shouldn't believe. Don't let the world tell you what's right and what's wrong. Don't let the world have any direction or influence in your life! In fact, you tell the world what's right and what's wrong! You tell the world what's good and what's bad! We're the lights of the world, and we're the salt of the earth. We're the ones who gives direction, light, and illumination because the world doesn't know.

"What is the renewing of your mind? Being born again and being born of the Word of God. A mind that has been washed and cleansed and acceptable unto God! Let me tell you something. Your mind can fool you. Your mind can make you think you are when you are not. I hate to say it, but for a lot of us in the church, our minds have fooled us. Our minds tells us we are when God's Word says, 'You are not!' Those are the people who gets mad with me. I know some you are going to get mad with me tonight. I know some are going to get mad, but God has given me this message and I'm going to give it to you! God said to watch your mind. Don't let your mind fool you! Don't let your mind trick you! Don't let your mind deceive you! Don't let your mind tell you you're all right when God's Word tells you you're wrong! Don't let your mind justify you when the Holy Ghost has already said it's wrong! Sometimes the preacher is preaching under the anointing of the Holy Ghost to the point that you can feel the conviction, but instead of turning to God, you walk right outside the church. Somebody said, 'I don't believe what he said. I don't think it takes all of that. I don't see it that way.' And then there's a whole lot of weak minded and silly folks who'll say 'You're right' and reject the Word of the Lord!

"What is the mind of Christ? The mind of Christ is the Word of God, and it agrees that the Word is right! Jesus always agreed with the Word of God. The mind of Christ always agrees with the Word of God even when it hurts the flesh to agree with it. Even if it's against my plan, my purpose, or my program. When you have the mind of Christ, you say Amen to the Word of God! If you're not saying Amen to the Word of God, then you don't have the mind of Christ. It has nothing to do with seeing or feeling. It's simply agreeing with the Word of God! As he approached the Garden of Gethsemane, Jesus himself had to go past his feelings and emotions to agree with the plan for his life. 'My soul is exceeding sorrowful, even unto death.... O my Father if it be possible, let this cup pass from me: nevertheless not as I will, but as thou wilt' (Matt. 26:38–39). He got up and said to his disciples, 'Rise up, let us go; lo he that betrayeth me is at hand' (Matt. 26:46).

"What is the mind of Christ? The mind of Christ will always walk within the way of God's holiness. There are too many of us who wants to make our own pathway. That's what a lot of you have done. The pathway you have made seems right to you and your fellow man, but in the end, it will turn out to be the way of death! You watch it! Some of you have rejected the old path and the old way of holiness according to the Word of God. You don't see that it is necessary, so you have created your own path. You think it is parallel to the old path, and you feel that it's so similar that it must end up at the same destination. But after a certain distance, your path reaches a precipice. The road to holiness is straight, it never varies, but your own path will go right over the precipice. The mind of Christ always stays within the way of God's holiness and righteousness. The mind of Christ always yields to the mind of Christ even when it means death. Most of us will fight, kick, scratch, and holler, 'No, Lord. No, no, no!' And you have the nerve to call yourself a Christian and full of the Holy Ghost. God says, 'You've got a long way to go.' The mind of Christ always follows the leading of the Holy Spirit."

Closing Prayer

"Come on. Stand on your feet and ask God to help you have the mind of Christ. Lord, help me have the mind of Christ. Renew my mind tonight. Deal with my spirit tonight. Whether it's lust, pride, flesh, the cares of this world—none of it is of God. God, you are warning us tonight, 'Watch your mind. Watch your mind. The enemy is playing with your mind. He hopes to deceive, destroy, and damn you! And he will, unless you watch your mind!' The Bible says, 'Thou wilt keep him in perfect peace, whose mind is stayed on thee: because he trusteth in thee.' God, work a miracle in here tonight. God, do something supernatural here tonight. God, get a hold of our minds and deal with our minds here on the altar. Some of us have to make new commitments and surrender our lives to you. Some of us have to denounce certain things we've been a part of, involved in, and even loving those things! We've got to make up our minds tonight. God is warning me! Unless I give this up and turn away from this, I will never be what He wants me to be, and He can never use me as He wants to use me, and I'll regret it throughout the countless ages of eternity. Now, Holy Spirit, do your awesome work here tonight in a supernatural manner we will never forget for the rest of our lives!

"I'm afraid there's a whole lot of folks in the church who have never been born again. I'm afraid there are too many folks who've simply recited a prayer and have never been truly born again. That's why if you're dealing with a soul at the altar, be sure that person has been born again before you tell them they are saved. Be sure they are willing to give themselves to the Lord and give up all their sins. For if they're not willing to give up their sins and give themselves to the Lord, they haven't been born again. You don't only have to believe Jesus Christ is the Son of God. You must be willing to belong to God, give up your sins, give up your unrighteousness, and give up the world! If you're not willing to do this, you'll never be born again."

Today, instead of identifying with the spirit of Christ, a high percentage of male churchgoers choose to identify with the world. Musicians in the house of the Lord are wearing earrings in one or both of their ears. I recently saw a picture of a well-known television evangelist wearing an earring in his ear. It's a crying shame, grieving the very spirit of God! Let God mold you. Let Him lead you in what you wear and how you should adorn yourself. Let God make you what he wants you to be! We were created for His pleasure! There have been many times when I've walked into a church and felt like I was a Pilgrim in any unholy land. I look at the preacher and the singers and instrumentalists, and I want to desperately ask them, 'Why are you here, and who and what do you seek? Is it the glory of God, or is it your own glory? Is your soul prepared for eternity? I know, beyond a shadow of doubt, if I died today, my soul is prepared. How's yours?'

Does your soul belong to Jesus? Is he truly the Lord of your life? The things that brings us pleasure may grieve the very heart of God! We need to make sure what brings us pleasure is one and the same with what pleases God. When you stand before the Lord on that great day, what will he say to you? What kind of excuses could you possibly give Him? Lord, I intercede on behalf of the entire church body. 'Choose ye this day whom you will serve.' You must choose wisely for the right choice will bring you life. Choose poorly, and your life will be taken from you. Make wise and godly choices of the people you surround yourself with. May it not be said, 'You stood up to be counted with the enemy!'

Jesus Christ is Lord

"The Lord has been doing marvelous things for these last three and half months. I came for just one week, with strength for only one week, but God has been strengthening me every day and in every service. We've seen one hundred or more baptized with the Holy Spirit in a supernatural outpouring. Bishop Caesar has been asking God, 'Lord, I want to see the Holy Ghost poured out.' God has poured it out until we hardly have anyone else left to receive the Holy Spirit. Over two hundred fifty persons have been baptized and saved. They've come to the altar and asked Christ to come into their hearts. Over fifty to sixty have joined the church. Now we want to make that one hundred. So I'm asking you to go home, rouse up somebody, kidnap somebody, or go bribe somebody … I don't care how you get them here. Get them here tonight! We want to see that number get to one hundred.

"How many of you got somebody that you know who is not saved, and you don't want to see them go to hell? Go and compel them to come and be with you in the service tonight. Some people you just have to pull and push, but bring them out to the service anyhow. Do whatever you got to do to get them here. I believe once you get them here, the Word of the Lord will convict their hearts, and they can be saved. So I'm asking everyone who can, to go and bring somebody to the service tonight. We're going to be praying for those who have special needs tonight. If you have a special need, God is a God who meets every special need you have, and he is going to work a miracle.

"Let's see if we can get enough people to take a vote to close the revival this week. We've been here three and a half months. I'm tired, and you're tired. So let's see if we can get some votes to close the revival. I see one little child with her hands raised along with mine to close the revival. All right, I guess the revival is going to go on for one more week. *Hallelujah*, one more week! I am certainly hoping you get your friends and your loved ones here this week starting on Wednesday night. Now we will be fasting all day Wednesday. It is important that you fast and pray! Let's meet here at the altar for prayer at seven in the evening.

"We've got to keep the prayer going because prayer always helps the revival. Wednesday night, we're going to pray for anyone who needs a miracle. So if you know anyone who needs a job, bring them to the service. Thursday night is Holy Spirit night. We're going to pray for those of you who want to know God's will for your life and receive his power. I believe God is going to do something supernatural, wonderful, and marvelous for you. If you believe it, say 'Amen.'

"Turn with me quickly to the Word of the Lord found in John 20:24–29:

"But Thomas, one of the twelve called Didymus, was not with them when Jesus came. The disciples said unto Him, 'We have seen the Lord.' But he said unto them, 'Except I shall see in his hands the print of the nails, and put my finger into the print of the nails, and thrust my hand into his side, I will not believe. And after eight days again his disciples were within, and Thomas with them: then came Jesus, the doors being shut, and stood in the midst, and said, 'Peace unto you.' Then saith he to Thomas, 'Reach hither thy finger, and behold my hands: and reach hither thy hand, and thrust it into my my side: and be not faithless, but believing.' And Thomas answered, 'My Lord and my God.' Jesus saith unto him, 'Thomas because thou hast seen me, thou hast believed: blessed are they that have not seen, and yet have believed.'"

"I want to talk briefly about Jesus Christ is Lord. How many of you believe that? Jesus Christ is Lord. I had a very unusual experience yesterday. The Lord spoke to my heart about this message. There are three things He said unto me: Jesus Christ is the Lord of repentance. He grants repentance to men and woman. In Acts 5:31, we have these words: 'Him hath God exalted with his right hand to be a Prince and a Savior, for to give repentance to Israel, and forgiveness of sins.'

"Jesus Christ has to grant you repentance, or else you will never be able to repent. Now the repentance Jesus Christ grants is a sorrow for sin. Not a sorrow for something that happened to you and you become sorrowful but a sorrow because you have realized you have broken God's law and his heart. Therefore, you owe God an apology. You've broken his heart, you've broken his law, and even though you may not have suffered any calamity, you've come to the realization that you were wrong! You, therefore, say to Him, 'I'm wrong. I repent. I ask you to forgive, and I am sorry. I'm so sorry that I'm going to quit.' Now that's the kind of repentance Jesus Christ gives. There are a whole lot of folks, sorry, but they're not going to quit.

"It's like you're driving down the freeway doing seventy-five miles per hour and the cops pull you over and say, 'Don't you know that you were speeding?'

"And you reply, 'Oh, officer, I'm so sorry. I wasn't looking at my speedometer. I am so sorry.'

"'Well, I'm going to let you go with a warning." Now you know that normally doesn't happen. They will usually give you a ticket. While you're watching him turn around and go back the opposite direction, in less than fifteen minutes, you're back up to seventy-five.

"You see, that's not repentance. You are sorry he caught you, but now you're back up to doing seventy-five. You're weren't really sorry. Jesus Christ grants you repentance because you see that you are wrong. I am wrong because God loves me, and God created me for himself. But I have rebelled against God, I have turned away from God, I went my own way, and I have gone against his statutes and followed my own will! Many people don't realize that it breaks the heart of God. It hurts God deeply.

"I had an experience with my son that illustrated that. I didn't know that doing wrong hurts God. My son asked me if he could be somewhere with his brother, and I said no. Now kids are smart. They'll ask their father for permission, and when he says no, then they go to their mother. She doesn't have good sense and will say yes. Now a woman with good sense will first say, 'What did your father say?' 'Well, Daddy said I can't go.' 'Well, that's it honey. If Daddy said you can't go, you can't go!'

"Some of you do worse by saying, 'Well, you go on. I'll take care of your daddy.' You don't ever tell a child that he can go on when his father said NO! Now if you think the father has made an unwise choice, you tell the child, 'You wait here, and I'll see if I can get Dad to change his mind.'

"You go to your husband and give him some facts he didn't know, or inform him of some things he may not have been thinking of. And then she'll say, 'In light of this, darling, sugar pie, sweetheart, and so forth, do you think it's all right for him to go?'

"And he'll say, 'Well, I didn't know all of that, and in view of all the facts, I think he can go.'

"Then you go back to the child, and say, 'Dad changed his mind, and you can go.' Then the child knows that both of you are together, and he will not be able to trick you or the mother. There are too many homes where the husband and wife are divided.

"Some of them are vying for the affection of the child, and the child gets away with murder. Children ought to be loved, and they ought to be disciplined. So I hollered in there to the boy and said, 'No, you can't go.' Then he went on anyhow. So when he came back, I sanctified him holy. I whipped him so. I just laid it on him. I believe when children disobey their parents, they ought to know 'You're going get something coming!'

"Some of y'all don't do nothing but promises. 'I'm going to get you. I'm going to get you!' You're lying. You ain't going to do nothing, and the child knows you're lying! You've been making those promises for a year, and the child says to himself, 'Ah, you ain't going to do nothing.' If you tell him you're going to get him, then get him!

Come on, Holy Ghost, help me now. So I sanctified him holy, and I put it on him! Today that boy is a preacher of the gospel!

"I went to church that night, and I didn't feel good. I felt terrible that the child deliberately disobeyed me. I went to church that night and said, 'Lord, I don't feel like preaching tonight. I don't feel like it! That child deliberately disobeyed me. He broke my heart! He hurt me way down in my soul, and I can't even scratch it and rub it! I'm just aching. I'm hurting!'

"God said to me, 'John, I know how you feel.'

"I said, 'How do you know how I feel? You don't have any hardheaded children like I got.' (Long pause)

"He said, 'You are my child, and you have disobeyed me. You don't realize it hurts me! Way down on the inside! Even though I am God, I can't scratch it, and I can't rub it! There's nothing I can do but suffer!'

"For the first time in my life, I saw that disobedience and sin hurts God. It breaks His heart! I looked up to God with tears in my eyes, and I said, 'Lord, forgive me! Don't ever let me disobey you again. Don't ever let me hurt you again the way I am hurting!' Sin hurts God. Disobedience hurts God. Stubbornness and rebellion hurts God. God gives you repentance and God wants you to repent, but so many of have said, 'I will not repent. I will not say I'm sorry.' Let me tell you something, if you don't repent, God has no other recourse but to destroy you. God offers you a chance to repent, to say I'm sorry, to ask for forgiveness, and to ask for a deliverance! But you get the devil in you and say, 'I will not.' Some children are just like that. You tell them, 'Say I'm sorry!'

"They'll say, 'I'm not going to say I'm sorry!' Well, if you don't say I'm sorry, I will make you sorry.

"God is speaking to someone here today. Jesus Christ offers you repentance. He's here to give you a spirit of repentance, a spirit of sorrow, a godly sorrow that makes you sorry enough to quit what you've been doing wrong. Now you can repent and be saved, or you can refuse and be damned. It's up to you! We've got to close this revival shortly, and the Holy Ghost has been saying throughout this whole revival, 'I'm giving you grace. I'm giving you time to repent. I'm giving you a chance to change, but when the revival closes, judgment is going to follow this revival if you have not repented.

"Some of you have sat there for three and half months and argued against everything Holy Ghost said through me. You've sat there and argued. You've sat there and rebutted. You went home and said, 'I don't care what John Lawrence said. I'm a person just like he is. I've got just as much sense as he got, and what he says means nothing.' Well, we're going to find out what it means. When the revival closes and you have not repented, I'm going to see what you're going to do with the judgment of God.

"You hear what God says. Night after night, the Holy Ghost has dealt with the homes. We've dealt with the homes. I said, 'Lord, I don't want to talk about the homes anymore. I don't want to talk about the family anymore.'

"God said, 'Talk about it!' There are homes that are messed up. There are homes where nobody wants to follow leadership and give respect and honor. Come on, Holy Ghost, help me. Stubborn and rebellious wives who don't want to obey, and be subject to their husbands. Who don't want to submit and don't want to be bothered! Husbands who don't want to love their wives as Christ loves the church or love their wives as their own bodies. Who don't want to give honor to the weaker vessel. God is saying, 'If you don't hear what I'm saying that when the revival is over, within a year's time, your marriage is going to break up, don't be calling out to me "Oh Lord" because I told you what to do, and you didn't do it.' Lift your hands and say, 'Lord, have mercy on my family.'

"This woman came to join the church, heard the gospel and the Lord spoke to her, and she went and got her husband! For a whole year, they had been separated. I thank God that she had sense enough to go get him. Some of y'all have put your husband out and don't have enough sense to go get him. 'Well, I just told him get on out!' Well, he ain't much of a man. I would tell you to get on out! I ain't going nowhere! I'm paying the rent, and you're going to put me out!

You must be crazy! 'I packed his stuff, child, and I put it outside the door.' I would have torn that door down! Set my stuff outside the door, and I'm paying the rent. I thought about what Jesus said, 'Go call your husband!' Those of you who have put him out, go call him. Ya hear! Go call him! 'The preacher said to call you. The Lord told him to tell you to come back home.'

"Some will say, 'Brother Lawrence, I got my pride.' What good is pride when you ain't got nothing else? Pride don't keep you warm at night. Pride don't comfort you. Pride don't share your troubles. You ain't nothing but a fool! 'My pride, my pride, I got my pride.' Well, somebody else got your man, and they're saying, 'Thank you' Jesus!' They are saying, 'Thank you Lord for her pride! Because of her pride, I got me a man!' Put your pride in your pocket, and go get your husband or your wife! Jesus said, 'Go call your husband, go get your husband, and bring him here. I got something for both of you. Go get him!'

"Now the Bible doesn't say whether she went and got him or not, but I believe if she had gone and got her husband, the Lord would have saved both of them. The Bible doesn't have a record of her getting the husband. It only records that she went and told the men of the city about Jesus. I believe if she had went and got him, the Lord would have saved the husband and reunited that home! He would have worked a miracle. I say to every woman that's separated from their husband, 'My God, Lord, have mercy. Go call him!' I won't say go get him because there may be someone out there ready to knock you in the head if you come to her house, talkin' about 'I'm here to get my husband.' You better call him on the telephone. Send him a mail gram. Forget your pride.

"'Well, my momma said …' Forget your momma! She ain't got nothing to do with your husband or you and your wife. "Well, my daddy said …' Forget your daddy! The Bible says to leave your father, leave your mother, join yourself to your husband, and become one flesh! And if God put you together, don't let nobody put you asunder. God is talking to someone here. Go get your husband this afternoon, if you can. Go call him, bring him in here this week. I believe God will put some homes together this week. How many of you believe that? Lift your hands and say, 'Lord, put some homes back together in the name of Jesus!' Now you go and get the husbands, go get the wives, and bring them here.

"The second thing the Lord said to me was he's 'the Lord of Regeneration.' I don't understand all of this, but he's 'the Lord of Regeneration.' In Matthew 19:28–29, Jesus says, 'Verily I say unto you, That ye which followed me, in the regeneration when the Son of man shall sit in the throne of his glory, ye also shall sit upon twelve thrones, judging the twelve tribes of Israel. And every one that hath forsaken houses, or father, or mother, or wife, or children, or lands, for my name's sake, shall receive an hundredfold, and shall inherit everlasting life.' God said to me, 'Jesus Christ is 'the Lord of Regeneration.' Now you can follow anybody. You can follow Allah or Buddha, but nobody can regenerate you but Jesus Christ!

"'Well, Brother Lawrence, they got this new religion.' Well, you can have it 'cause I don't want it. I want a God who can change me inside *out* and outside *in*. The Bible says, 'If any man be in Christ, he is a new creature.' What has happened? Jesus Christ has regenerated that man, woman, boy, or girl and made a new creature out of them! Nobody can do that but Jesus Christ. 'What are you talking about?' I'm talking about this. If you used to be a liar, He'll take the *lying* out of your tongue and make you speak the *truth*.

"I used to be an "A" number one liar, but I got saved. God took the *lying* out and put the *truth* in. I mean if you're a thief and you steal, He'll take the *stealing* out. The Bible says, 'Let him that stole, steal no more.' If you put it down, before I was saved, if you blink, I'll take it while you're looking at it. But when He regenerated me, brother, you could put it down, and you don't have to worry about it because I'm not going to bother it.

"I used to work for a Jewish man, and at Christmas time, when I really needed some money, he'd drop twenty dollars on the floor to see if I was going to take it. Now I know no Jewish man will actually drop twenty dollars. So I'd be sweeping and come up on this twenty dollar bill, and the devil would say, 'Look here, man. You sure are blessed today. Here's twenty dollars on the floor. Now pick it up, put it your pocket, and say no more.'

"I'd say, 'You're a liar. It's not mine.' So I'd pick it up, take it up to my boss, and say, 'Mr. Kleinzeller.'

"'Yeah, John?'

"'Here's the twenty dollars you put on the floor to see if I would steal it. I don't steal!' He tried every way he could to tempt me to steal. The day I preached my trial sermon, that Jewish man, his son-in-law, and his grandson were sitting in our converted garage church to hear me preach. And I preached that Jesus Christ is truly the son of God. I told the story, but I shut my eyes because I didn't want to see him. I thought, for sure, he was going to fire me because I talked about Jesus that day. When I got back to work the next day, he said, 'I've never seen someone speak like that before. You just went into a trance.' I wasn't in no trance. I just didn't want look to at his face while I was talking about Jesus. Jesus Christ will regenerate you to the point that whatever it is that you used to do wrong, you don't want to do anymore! You'll give that up, you'll put that down, and you will let that go because Jesus Christ is 'the Lord of regeneration.'

"If you say, 'Brother Lawrence, I've been regenerated, but I keep doing wrong.' Well, there's something wrong with your regeneration. There's something wrong with your commitment, your surrender, because when Jesus Christ does a job, he does a good job! I don't care what it is. I don't care if you're a homosexual, I don't care if you're a lesbian, I don't care if you're a dope addict, I don't care if you're an alcoholic, I don't care if you're a gambler, I don't care what it *is!* If you'll kneel at this altar and say to Jesus Christ, 'I totally surrender. I completely surrender my entire self to you.' I guarantee you Jesus Christ will work a work of regeneration in you so completely, so totally, that you'll never be the same again. Do I have any witnesses in here? Then say *Amen!*

"Jesus Christ will save you, he'll convert you, and he'll give you a new birth. You can be born again. Now turning over a new leaf is not the same thing. That's *you* turning over a new leaf, and the new leaf turns out to be just like the old one. But if Jesus Christ turns you over, turns you around, and turns you *inside out*, you can live holy, you can love God, and you can walk with Jesus Christ.

"Jesus Christ is 'the Lord of righteousness.' In 1 Peter 2:21–22: 'For even hereunto were ye called: because Christ also suffered for us, leaving us an example, that ye should follow his steps: Who did no sin, neither was guile found in his mouth.' Jesus did no sin. He is righteous, and if you are in Him, you are righteous. He is 'the Lord of righteousness.' That's why I can't understand these people who say they are charismatic. They can still drink, commit adultery, lie, and steal. Somebody is lying somewhere. If you're a child of God, then the old life, *you give it up, you turn it loose, you let it go, you give yourself totally to God, and you will love righteousness.*

"1 John 3:7 speaks about that: 'Little children, let no man deceive you: he that doeth righteousness is righteous, even as he is righteous.' Jesus Christ is right and never wrong. Jesus Christ is truth and never a lie. Jesus Christ is holy and never unholy. He is the Lord of righteousness.

"Now, anytime anybody tells you they're a follower of Jesus Christ and their life does not measure up to righteousness, don't believe it. Folks will say, 'Well, if that's Christianity, then I don't want it.' That's not Christianity. If you see something wrong, or your brother doing wrong, that person is wrong, not Jesus Christ and not the righteousness God offers or the righteousness that he gives. That person is wrong, and the reason that person is wrong is because Satan is controlling that person. When God controls you, *you'll live right, you'll live holy, you'll live godly, and you'll live right.* Come on, Holy Ghost, help me just a little bit here.

"Jesus Christ is the Lord of righteousness. He will help you live righteously, godly, soberly, and holy right down here in this present world. 'Brother Lawrence, when I get to heaven, I'm going to live right.' If you don't do some right living before you get there, *you won't get there.* You've got to practice and perfect it here, or God will never allow you there. There are some preachers who espouse a theology that everybody sins, and there's no one living right.

"They say it's like an apple on a tree that falls from the tree when it ripens. When a person gets to that ripened level of righteousness, they'll drop off and die. The truth about that is this: *the preacher is a crook.* He wants something to cloak his crookedness, so he'll tell you no one can live right. So if you catch him drinking, drunk, or with one of the sisters committing adultery, he'll say, 'I told you nobody can live right, didn't I?' Now see, that's a crook. If nobody can live right, if you can't help me to do right, then I don't need you to do wrong. I can do that by myself. I don't want the church, preacher, or anybody to help me do wrong. I need someone to tell me about *living right, living holy, living godly, and living like Jesus!* Now if the preacher can't do that for you, then he's no good for you. Come on, Holy Ghost!

"Last thing, then I'll conclude. I heard the Holy Spirit say to me, 'Jesus Christ is the Lord of resurrection.' This thrills me. I don't care how hopeless the case is. Jesus Christ is the Lord of the resurrection. When He came into the home of Lazarus, Mary, and Martha, Martha, in so many words, was rebuking Jesus. 'Lord, had you been here he would not have died. What took you so long? I sent you a notice early enough that you could have made it before he died.'

"Jesus said, 'You'll see your brother again.'

"'I know. I know I'll see him in the resurrection. I'll see him when all of the saints get up out of the grave, and meet God in the air.'

"Jesus said, 'I am the resurrection and the life. Where have you lain him?' They then took Him to the grave.

"This is what proves that Jesus was God Almighty. Most preachers and religious leaders would have gone there and said, 'Oh, Lazarus, my friend, I'm so sorry I didn't make it here in time, but I'll pay you my last respects. I'm leaving some flowers for you. To let you know we sympathize with you, and we miss you.' Then they would have gone back home and went to bed. But Jesus said, 'Show me the place where you've lain him.' They had rolled a big stone there because of the corruption. Jesus said, 'Move the stone.'

"Mary said, 'He's been dead for four days, and by now, he stinketh.'

"Jesus said, 'Didn't I tell you to believe, and you'll see the glory of God.' They removed the stone. Jesus looked up and said, 'Father, I thank you that you always hear me.' I really believe He said, 'Now we agreed on this last night. Everything is ready? All right, okay!' Then Jesus yelled, 'Lazarus!'

"Somebody said, 'What is He doing?'

"Someone replied, 'He's calling Lazarus!'

"'What is He calling Lazarus for? I was there when Lazarus died, and he's dead. So there's no need for him to be calling Lazarus." But he didn't know who was calling Lazarus.

"'Lazarus!'

"Somebody said, 'You're wasting your breath, man. He's been in there four days. I was there when they put him there. It's too late. The worms got him now. So just forget it. Let's go home and eat some chicken or something because there's no sense for being here.'

"Jesus said, 'Lazarus, come on outta there!'

"Somebody said, 'I don't believe this. I think Jesus done flipped his lid, calling a dead man to come out!' But then they heard some noise, feet shuffling.

"Somebody said, 'What's that noise? Sounds like somebody walking.'

"Another said, 'Let me get on outta here.'

"Less than a few minutes later, Lazarus stood at the door. *Hallelujah, hallelujah!* You can be sure a lot of those folks took off and started running. Jesus said, 'Loose him. Take off those wrappings around him. Get those clothes off of him, loose him, and let him go!'

"Jesus Christ is the Lord of the Resurrection. It doesn't matter how hopeless the case is. It doesn't matter how difficult the situation is. It doesn't matter how impossible things are. If Jesus Christ is your Lord, all you got to do is speak the word and things come back together again. All you got to do is make a call, and the situation changes. *Good God, have mercy!* Somebody said, 'Why are you a Christian? Why aren't you a Muslim? Why aren't you a Buddhist?' I am Christian because Jesus is *the Lord of the Resurrection.* I'm not going trust Buddha because Buddha can't call me back once I'm gone.

I'm not going to trust Allah because I don't have any proof that Allah can bring me back when I'm gone. I put my trust in Jesus because he has already proven he is the Lord of the Resurrection! He called a man back from the grave that was dead for four days. Then He said something else, 'No man takes my life.' He said, 'I lay it down.'

"Folks said, 'You're going to lay it down? What do you mean?'

"He said, 'I'm going to die!'

"They said, 'So what are we going to do?'

"He said, 'I'll make you a promise. In three days, I'm going to rise again.'

"'Now let's get this straight. You're going to die. You're going to be in a grave for three days and three nights, and you're going to get up out of the grave and come back?'

"'Yes.'

"'You sure?'

"As Jonah was in the belly of the fish for three days and three nights, so will the Son of Man be in the hallowed earth for three days and three nights. And just like Jesus said, they crucified him, put him in the tomb, put soldiers around the tomb to be sure no one will go in there and steal him, and in case anyone tries to come out there to get him. Three days and three nights passed. Then an earthquake came and shook things to pieces, and the soldiers who were guarding the tomb fell out like dead men. Then angels came and sat there. *Hallelujah!* Jesus got up and came out of the grave. He said, 'I lay my life down and pick it up again. This commandment I have of my Father.'

"This proves Jesus Christ is Lord because not only did he raise a man from the grave, he died himself, and at end of three days and three nights, he got up out of the grave. And He made this statement, 'All powers are given into my hands, in the heavens, and in the earth. Go ye into all the world, and preach the gospel to every creature. He that believeth and is baptized shall be saved! He that believeth not shall be damned.'"

John's Altar Call

"Come on and stand with me. Lift your hands and say, 'Thank God for Jesus.' Thank you Jesus. You are the Lord of regeneration; Lord of the resurrection. God, even though we may die, you have made the promise that those who are in the grave will hear your voice and have the hope that Jesus Christ is going to resurrect us from the dead. Father, every man, every woman, every boy, and every girl, this day, you've said to them that Jesus Christ is Lord.

"He is the Lord of repentance, and if you will allow Him, today, He'll grant repentance to you. John 6:65 says, "Therefore I have said to you that no one can come to Me unless it has been granted to him by My Father." Jesus Christ has to give you that repentance. If He doesn't give it to you, you'll never repent. And He's offering it to you now. He cannot guarantee you'll have tomorrow. He cannot guarantee you'll have it just before you die. He said, 'Today, if you would hear my voice, harden not your hearts.' (Psalm 95:7, 8) Father, today you are speaking to every sinner, backslider, hypocrite, every man, woman, boy, and girl in this audience. You're saying, 'Jesus Christ, my son, is Lord. And through Him, He offers repentance to you today.' Through *Him,* you are offering regeneration today. Through *Him,* you're offering righteousness today. Through *Him,* you are offering the promise of resurrection. But if you *reject Him,* you will be damned. You have no hope in this world or the world to come. Lord, have mercy here today. Touch the heart of every man, every

146

woman, every boy, and every girl. Touch the heart of every back-slider, every hypocrite, and every person out of fellowship with God today. Convict them of their sins and the works of the power of the enemy. Let them repent right now.

"Every sinner, every person not right with God, every backslider, I want you to lift your hands and say, 'Preacher, pray for me. I'm not right with God. If I die right now, I'll go to hell because I've made no preparation for eternity. Jesus Christ is not my Lord. I haven't repented of my sins. I haven't been made righteous by Him. If I die right now, I have no promise of being in the first resurrection.' You say, 'Brother Lawrence, I've joined the church.' That's not enough. You've got to be born again. You say, 'I'm a pretty decent person.' That's not good enough. You've got to be born *again.* I'm not asking you to join the church. I'm asking you to let Jesus Christ become your Lord today, to let him rule over your life, and to take control of you! You're here today, and God is stretching out his hands. Tomorrow you may be in judgment. Hell is hot, and eternity is a *long time!*

"Father, in the name of Jesus, every sinner, every backslider, every person that's out of fellowship with you today, Jesus Christ is not their Lord and not their Savior. I pray for them right now. I pray that you'll forgive them of their sins. I pray that you regenerate them. *O God,* convict them of their sins, their wrongdoings, and change their life. Make them righteous, godly, *holy!* Bring them to the foot of the cross. Let them accept *Jesus Christ* as their Savior. Then give them the promise of the resurrection. They will be in that first res-urrection where the righteous will get up, children of God will get up, and those with hope will *get up!* The last resurrection is for the damned. When they get up, it's too late to do anything but cry! Too late to do anything but *scream.* For God's mercy will be clean, gone forever. God's grace will be clean gone forever! There will be nothing or no one you can appeal to! There will be no need to cry for mercy, for mercy will have stepped aside, and justice will be sitting on the throne. No need to be talking about forgiveness because it will have gone out of business. It will be *too late* to be forgiven.

"God, have mercy today. Father, in the name of Jesus, I pray for my brother today. O God, have mercy on him today! Forgive him today! Regenerate him today! Make a child of God out of him today. Supernaturally, I pray in Jesus's mighty name. I break the power of sin, the power of Satan, and every habit and *addiction,* and I command a *deliverance in Jesus's name."*

John Lawrence once remarked, "Prayer is the key to revival. When the saints begin to pray, God begins to move!" I recently spoke to a dear friend and asked her if the church she attends still has all-night prayer. When she replied no, it just broke my heart.

David Jeremiah offered this commentary on our present-day church. "People ask, 'Why has the church lost its influence?' We have become so fixated on being relevant that we have become totally irrelevant. We have become so fixated on taking our mantra from the media and taking our marching orders from the market place, instead of from the Word of God, that we now have nothing to say to the world that's different from what they can get just about any place else. So when we no longer are *the church in the world,* why should we expect the world to ever come and ask what we think about anything! There's time for us to get back. Maybe, this is the time. Toleration is a word that's being overlooked. There is a toleration, which is treachery, and there is a peace, which is paralysis. Ladies and gentlemen, we are walking into a period of time that is very Pergamenian (Rev. 2:14). Where, if we're not careful, we are going to lose our sense of who we are, and the church will be just a byword as it has become already in so many places. So what do we do about it?"

Let's consider the consequences of the effectual prayers of the righteous. I believe God would move mightily if the body of Christ would, consistently, call for days or weeks of prayer and fasting. All requests that affects our nation and nations around the world would be brought before the throne of God. Can you imagine if the entire body of Christ from every nation in the world would earnestly pray for the removal of wickedness in high places and for a worldwide revival?

While I rejoice that heaven is now his home, I am saddened because John Lawrence is tremendously missed. We don't hear about revivals where people are getting saved and filled with the Holy Ghost, deliverances from all kinds of addictions and habits, family curses are lifted, and entire churches are changed forever! I'm talking about *true revival!* No one has taken the mantle. He is, without question, the greatest evangelist/soul winner I've encountered in my life. When you consider the number of people who were saved under his revivals and soul winning crusades, it wouldn't surprise me if millions of lives were affected by the ministry of this powerful servant of God.

My Prayer

O GOD, IN JESUS'S NAME, ON behalf of the true body of Christ, I bring to you our deepest yearnings—to be good, faithful servants, giving you our very best at all times. I am asking you to fix us, Lord. May we be willing to allow you to mold us into the vessels you want us to be. In Second Corinthians 7:1, your servant Paul exhorted, "Let us cleanse ourselves from all filthiness of the flesh and spirit, perfecting holiness in the fear of God." Lord, I know it grieves your heart when you see preachers and laymen living unholy lives, committing sins that are *abominations* in your eyes. May they become disgusted of their sins and desperately seek deliverances from their sins and healing for their souls. As Pastor David Jeremiah once prayed, "We ask you Lord to make us vigilant. We ask you Lord to give us courage. We ask you to help us understand that we can still be the church. If people want to ridicule us and say we're intolerant as we speak the truth, so be it. But when we speak the truth, we stand in the train of the Lord God, who called us to truth."

Raise up, men and women of God, who will live sanctified holy lives. Let us be examples for the young and old. May the true worshippers, those who are baptized in the Holy Ghost, filled with the fullness of God, stand up and *be counted!* May the world be drawn to you, Jesus, by the lifestyles and testimonies of your sons and daughters. Let the world revival that John Lawrence spoke of come forth sovereignly, mightily, and according to your divine will and timetable. Amen!

About the Author

EDGAR A. MEEKS IS A musician, teacher, preacher, and freelance writer born and raised on Long Island, New York. *Crying Loud and Sparing Not*, his first book, contains the essence of the late great evangelist John Lawrence's incredible ministry, which spanned nearly five decades, highlighted by the great revival of 1984 held at Bethel Gospel Tabernacle in Jamaica, New York. He was simply a country preacher, great soul winner, and marriage counselor, effectively advancing the Kingdom of God.

CPSIA information can be obtained
at www.ICGtesting.com
Printed in the USA
BVHW012113060420
577054BV00004B/175